C O U N T R Y
Pubs & Inns of
SUSSEX

By Peter Long

Regional Hidden Places

Cornwall
Devon
Dorset, Hants & Isle of Wight
East Anglia
Gloucs, Wiltshire & Somerset
Heart of England
Hereford, Worcs & Shropshire
Lake District & Cumbria
Lancashire & Cheshire
Northumberland & Durham
Peak District
Sussex
Yorkshire

National Hidden Places

England
Ireland
Scotland
Wales

Hidden Inns

East Anglia
Heart of England
North of England
South
South East
West Country
Yorkshire

Country Pubs & Inns

Cornwall
Devon
Sussex
Yorkshire
Wales

Country Living
Rural Guides

East Anglia
Heart of England
Ireland
North East of England
North West of England
Scotland
South
South East
Wales
West Country

Published by: Travel Publishing Ltd, 7a Apollo House, Calleva Park, Aldermaston, Berkshire RG7 8TN

ISBN 1-904-43436-3

© Travel Publishing Ltd

Published 2006

Printing by: Scotprint, Haddington

Maps by: © Maps in Minutes ™ (2006)
© Crown Copyright, Ordnance Survey 2006

Editor: Peter Long

Cover Design: Lines and Words, Aldermaston, Berkshire

Cover Photograph: The Thatched Tavern, East Wittering, Sussex

Text Photographs: © www.britainonview.com

Foreword

The *Country Pubs & Inns of Sussex* is one of a series of guides which will eventually cover the whole of the UK. This guide provides details of pubs and inns (including hotels which welcome non-residents) situated in the countryside of Sussex. "Countryside" is officially defined by *The Office of National Statistics* as "settlements of less than 10,000 inhabitants".

There are of course many selectively-based pub guides covering the UK but each title in the Country Pubs & Inns series will provide the reader with the *most comprehensive* choice of pubs and inns in the countryside through handy-sized, county-based guides. The guide enables the reader to choose the pub or inn to visit based on his/her own criteria such as location, real ales served, food, entertainment etc.

This easy-to-use guide is divided into 6 chapters which allows the reader to select the area of Sussex being visited. Each chapter begins with a map containing the numbered location of the pub or inn and a brief illustrated summary of the places of interest in the area. By using the number the reader can then find more information on their choice of pub or inn.

We do hope that you will enjoy visiting the pubs and inns contained in this guide. We are always interested in what our readers think of the pubs and inns covered (or not covered) in our guides so please do not hesitate to write to us using the reader reaction forms provided to the rear of the guide. Equally, you may contact us via our email address at info@travelpublishing.co.uk. This is a vital way of ensuring that we continue to provide a comprehensive list of pubs and inns to our readers.

Finally, if you are seeking visitor information on Sussex or any other part of the British Isles we would like to refer you to the full list of Travel Publishing guides to be found at the rear of the book. You may also find more information about any of our titles on our website at www.travelpublishing.co.uk

Travel Publishing

How to use the guide

The *Country Pubs & Inns of Sussex* provides details of pubs and inns (including hotels which welcome non-residents) situated in the countryside of Sussex. "Countryside" is defined by *The Office of National Statistics* as "settlements of less than 10,000 inhabitants" so much of Sussex fulfills this definition!

This guide has been specifically designed as an easy-to-use guide so there is no need for complicated instructions. However the reader may find the following guidelines helpful in identifying the name, address, telephone number and facilities of the pub or inn.

Finding Pubs or Inns in a Selected Location

The guide is divided into 6 chapters (or sections) each covering a specific geographical area of Sussex. Identify the area and page number you require from the map and table of contents on the following pages and turn to the relevant chosen page.

At the beginning of each chapter there is a detailed map of the area selected. The villages and towns denoted by **red** circles are places of interest on which information is provided in the introduction to the chapter should you wish to explore the area further. The numbered boxes in green represent each pub or inn in the area selected. For more information on the pub or inn simply locate the same number within the chapter (to the left of the pub/inn name) to find the name, address, telephone number and facilities of the pub or inn.

Finding a Specific Pub or Inn

If you know the name of the pub or inn and its location then simply go to the relevant chapter where the names of the pubs are listed in alphabetical order.

Pub and Inn Information

All pubs or inns in the guide give details of the name, address, telephone number and whether they offer real ales, food, accommodation and no smoking areas.

The advertising panels found in each chapter provide more comprehensive information on the pub or inn such as contact details, location, interior and exterior facilities, real ales, opening times, food, entertainment, disabled access, credit cards and places of interest.

Location Map

BERKSHIRE

SURREY

KENT

HAMPSHIRE   **Section 5**   **Section 3**   **Section 1**

W. SUSSEX   E. SUSSEX

Section 6   **Section 4**   **Section 2**

Contents

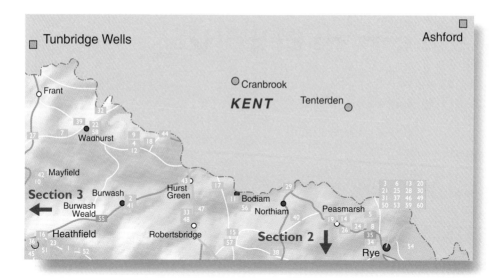

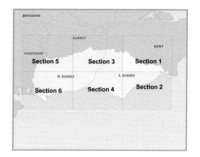

11	Pub or Inn Reference Number - Detailed Information
12	Pub or Inn Reference Number - Summary Entry
● ■	Place of interest mentioned in the chapter introduction

EAST SUSSEX – HEATHFIELD TO RYE

The chief towns and villages in this area bordering Kent are Burwash (Bateman's was the home for many years of Rudyard Kipling), Northiam (Brickwall House and Great Dixter House are the grand houses here), Hurst Green, Bodiam, Robertsbridge and Wadhurst, once a centre of the iron industry. Perhaps the most historic and picturesque of all is Rye, a founding member of the Confederacy of the Cinque Ports.

Bodiam

Bodiam Castle, one of the most romantic in the country, was begun in 1385. After a long period of decay, restoration of this moated castle started at the end of the 19th century and was completed by Lord Curzon in 1919. Bodiam is on the steam-operated **Kent & East Sussex Railway**.

Burwash

Just outside this one-time centre of the iron industry stands **Bateman's**, a sandstone Jacobean house that was the home from 1902 to Rudyard Kipling. Both the house, kept as it was in Kipling's time, and the 33-acre grounds landscaped by the writer and his wife, are well worth exploring.

Northiam

Northiam is on the **Kent & East Sussex Railway**,

which was restored in 1990 and operates steam trains between Tenterden in Kent and Bodiam during the summer months. In the village is the imposing 17th century **Brickwall House**, while nearby lies **Great Dixter House**, a late-medieval house with the largest timber-framed hall in the country. The gardens are among the finest in the land.

Great Dixter House and Gardens, Northiam

Rye

This old and very picturesque town was originally granted to the Abbey of Fecamp in Normandy in 1027, and was only reclaimed by Henry III in 1247. It became a member of the Confederacy of the Cinque Ports and grew prosperous in the late medieval period due to the

The Quay, Rye

activities of its fishermen and the merchant fleets that traded with Europe. One of four gateways in the perimeter wall is **Landgate** – all that remains of the fortifications built by Edward III in the 1340s. One of Rye's oldest buildings is **Ypres Tower**, now part of the **Rye Castle Museum**. **Lamb House** was the home of Henry James, who wrote some of his best-known works while living here.

Wadhurst

The **Church of St Peter and St Paul** has a unique collection of iron tomb slabs marking the graves of local ironmasters who died in the area between 1617 and 1772.

1 The Barley Mow
Punnetts Town, Heathfield, East Sussex TN21 9DL
Tel: 01435 831520
Real Ales, Bar Food, Restaurant Menu,
No Smoking Area, Disabled Facilities

2 The Bear Inn & Burwash Motel
High St, Burwash, Etchingham,
East Sussex TN19 7ET
Tel: 01435 882540
Real Ales, Bar Food, Restaurant Menu,
Accommodation, No Smoking Area, Disabled Facilities

3 Bedford Arms
91 Fishmarket Rd, Rye, East Sussex TN31 7LR
Tel: 01797 224867
Real Ales

4 The Bell Hotel
High St, Ticehurst, Wadhurst, East Sussex TN5 7AS
Tel: 01580 200234
Real Ales, Disabled Facilities

5 Bell Inn
Church Lane, Iden, Rye, Sussex TN31 7XD
Tel: 01797 280242
Real Ales, Bar Food, Restaurant Menu,
Accommodation, No Smoking Area

6 Benson Hotel
15 East Street, Rye, Sussex TN31 7JY
Tel: 01797 225131
Restaurant Menu, Accommodation, No Smoking Area

7 Best Beech Inn
Mayfield Lane, Wadhurst, Sussex TN5 6JH
Tel: 01892 782046
Real Ales, Bar Food, Restaurant Menu,
Accommodation, No Smoking Area, Disabled Facilities

8 Broomhill Lodge Hotel
Peasmarsh Road, Rye, Sussex TN31 7UN
Tel: 01797 280421
Accommodation, No Smoking Area, Disabled Facilities

9 Bull Inn
Three Leg Cross, Ticehurst, Wadhurst,
Sussex TN5 7HH
Tel: 01580 200586
Real Ales, Bar Food, Accommodation,
No Smoking Area

10 The Carpenters Arms
Fletching Street, Mayfield, Sussex TN20 6TB
Tel: 01435 873294
Real Ales, Bar Food, Restaurant Menu,
No Smoking Area

11 Castle Inn
Main Street, Bodian, Robertsbridge,
Sussex TN32 5UB
Tel: 01580 830330
Real Ales, Bar Food, Restaurant Menu,
No Smoking Area

12 The Chequers Inn
High Street, Wadhurst, Sussex TN5 7BQ
Tel: 01580 200287
Real Ales, No Smoking Area

13 Cinque Ports Hotel
Cinque Ports Street, Rye, Sussex TN31 7AN
Tel: 01797 222319
Real Ales, Bar Food, Restaurant Menu,
Accommodation, Disabled Facilities

14 Cock Horse
Main Street, Peasmarsh, Rye, Sussex TN31 6YD
Tel: 01797 230281
Real Ales, Bar Food, Restaurant Menu

15 Cross Inn The
Cripps Corner Road, Robertsbridge,
Sussex TN32 5QA
Tel: 01580 830217
Real Ales

16 The Crown Inn
Burwash Road, Heathfield, Sussex TN21 8RA
Tel: 01435 867491
Real Ales, Bar Food, Restaurant Menu,
No Smoking Area, Disabled Facilities

17 Curlew

Junction Road, Bodiam, Robertsbridge,
Sussex TN32 5UY
Tel: 01580 861394

Real Ales, Bar Food, Restaurant Menu,
No Smoking Area

18 Dale Hill Hotel & Golf Club

Ticehurst, Wadhurst, Sussex TN5 7DQ
Tel: 01580 200112

Real Ales, Bar Food, Restaurant Menu,
Accommodation, Disabled Facilities

19 Flackley Ash Hotel

Peasmarsh, Rye, Sussex TN31 6YH
Tel: 01797 230651

Real Ales, Bar Food, Restaurant Menu,
Accommodation, No Smoking Area, Disabled Facilities

20 Frenches Wine Bar

The Strand, Rye, Sussex TN31 7DB
Tel: 01797 227080

Real Ales

21 The Globe Inn

10 Military Rd, Rye, East Sussex TN31 7NX
Tel: 01797 227918

Real Ales, Bar Food, Restaurant Menu, No Smoking Area

22 The Greyhound

St. James Square, High Street, Wadhurst,
Sussex TN5 6BH
Tel: 01892 783224

Real Ales, Bar Food, Restaurant Menu,
Accommodation, No Smoking Area, Disabled Facilities

23 The Half Moon Inn

Cade St, Heathfield, East Sussex TN21 9BS
Tel: 01435 868646

Real Ales, Bar Food, Restaurant Menu

24 The Hare & Hounds

Rye Road, Rye, Sussex TN31 7ST
Tel: 01797 230483

Real Ales, Bar Food, Restaurant Menu,
Accommodation, No Smoking Area, Disabled Facilities

25 Hope Anchor Hotel

Watchbell Street, Rye, Sussex TN31 7HA
Tel: 01797 222216

Real Ales, Bar Food, Restaurant Menu,
Accommodation, No Smoking Area

26 Horse & Cart

School Lane, Peasmarsh, Rye, Sussex TN31 6UW
Tel: 01797 230220

Real Ales, Bar Food, Restaurant Menu, No Smoking
Area, Disabled Facilities

27 The Mark Cross Inn

Mark Cross, Crowborough, Sussex TN6 3NP
Tel: 01892 852423

Real Ales, Bar Food, Restaurant Menu,
No Smoking Area, Disabled Facilities

28 Mermaid Inn

Mermaid Street, Rye, Sussex TN31 7EU
Tel: 01797 223065

Real Ales, Bar Food, Restaurant Menu,
Accommodation, No Smoking Area

29 The Mill

Station Road, Northiam, Rye, Sussex TN31 6QT
Tel: 01797 252999

Real Ales, Bar Food, Restaurant Menu,
No Smoking Area, Disabled Facilities

30 The Monastery

6 High Street, Rye, Sussex TN31 7JE
Tel: 01797 223272

Restaurant Menu, No Smoking Area

31 The Old Bell

High Street, Rye, Sussex TN31 7EN
Tel: 01797 223323

Real Ales, Bar Food, No Smoking Area

32 The Old Vine

Wadhurst, Sussex TN5 6ER
Tel: 01892 782271

Real Ales, Bar Food, Restaurant Menu,
No Smoking Area

33 Ostrich Hotel
Station Road, Robertsbridge, Sussex TN32 5DG
Tel: 01580 881737

Real Ales, Bar Food, Restaurant Menu,
Accommodation, No Smoking Area

34 Peace & Plenty
Rye Road, Playden, Rye, Sussex TN31 7UL
Tel: 01797 280342

Real Ales, Bar Food, Restaurant Menu,
No Smoking Area, Disabled Facilities

35 Playden Oasts Inn
Rye Road, Rye, Sussex TN31 7UL
Tel: 01797 223502

Real Ales, Bar Food, Restaurant Menu,
Accommodation, No Smoking Area

See panel below

36 Prince Of Wales
Hailsham Road, Heathfield, Sussex TN21 8DR
Tel: 01435 862919

Real Ales, Bar Food, Restaurant Menu,
Accommodation, No Smoking Area, Disabled Facilities

37 The Queens Restaurant
The Queens Head Hotel, Rye, Sussex TN31 7LH
Tel: 01797 222181

Real Ales, Restaurant Menu, Accommodation,
No Smoking Area

38 Rainbow Trout Inn
Chitcombe Road, Broad Oak, Brede,
Sussex TN31 6EU
Tel: 01424 882436

Real Ales, Bar Food, Restaurant Menu,
No Smoking Area, Disabled Facilities

---

35 The Playden Oasts Inn
Rye Road, Playden, nr Rye, East Sussex TN31 7UL
☎ 01797 223502 ⊕ www.playdenoasts.co.uk

**Real Ales, Bar Food, Restaurant Menu,
Accommodation, No Smoking Area**

- On the main A268 Playden-Rye road 1 mile from Rye centre
- Harveys Best Bitter
- 12-3 & evening to 9
- 8 en suite rooms
- Garden, terrace, car park
- Major cards accepted
- 12-11.30
- Rye 1 mile, Northiam (Great Dixter Garden, Steam Railway) 5 miles

Many of the traditional oast houses of Kent and Sussex have found new roles, but none have been more attractively converted than the **Playden Oasts**. This small hotel, pub and restaurant run by Bob and Raphaele stands just a mile from the centre of Rye and four miles from the beach at Camber Sands. The comfortable, civilised bar, situated in one of the creeper-clad roundels, serves a wide range of beers, wines and spirits, and in the two restaurants the chef makes excellent use of the best seasonal produce in classic dishes that include fish freshly landed by local boats. Playden Oasts has eight characterful bedrooms, all with en suite facilities, television, tea/coffee trays and hairdryers. The inn has a delightful garden and ample off-road parking.

39 Red Lion Public House
Wadhurst, Sussex TN5 6ST
Tel: 01892 782628

Real Ales, Bar Food, Restaurant Menu,
No Smoking Area, Disabled Facilities

40 Rose & Crown
Northiam Road, Beckley, Rye, Sussex TN31 6SE
Tel: 01797 252161

Real Ales, Bar Food, Restaurant Menu,
No Smoking Area, Disabled Facilities

41 Rose & Crown Inn
Ham Lane, Burwash, Etchingham, Sussex TN19 7ER
Tel: 01435 882600

Real Ales, Bar Food, Restaurant Menu,
Accommodation, No Smoking Area, Disabled Facilities

42 Rose & Crown Inn
Fletching Street, Mayfield, Sussex TN20 6TE
Tel: 01435 872200

Real Ales, Bar Food, Restaurant Menu,
Accommodation, No Smoking Area

43 The Royal George
London Rd, Hurst Green, Etchingham,
East Sussex TN19 7PN
Tel: 01580 860200

Real Ales, Bar Food, Restaurant Menu,
No Smoking Area, Disabled Facilities

44 The Royal Oak
London Road , Flimwell, Wadhurst,
East Sussex TN5 7PJ
Tel: 01580 879630

Real Ales, Bar Food, Restaurant Menu,
No Smoking Area, Disabled Facilities

45 Runt In Tun
Maynards Green, Sussex TN21 0DJ
Tel: 01435 864284

Real Ales, Bar Food, Restaurant Menu,
No Smoking Area

46 Rye Lodge Hotel
Hilders Cliff, Rye, Sussex TN31 7LD
Tel: 01797 223838

Restaurant Menu, Accommodation,
No Smoking Area, Disabled Facilities

47 Salehurst Halt
Church Lane, Salehurst, Robertsbridge,
Sussex TN32 5PH
Tel: 01580 880620

Real Ales, Restaurant Menu, No Smoking Area,
Disabled Facilities

48 Seven Stars Inn
High Street, Robertsbridge, Sussex TN32 5AJ
Tel: 01580 880333

Real Ales, Bar Food, Restaurant Menu,
No Smoking Area

49 The Ship Inn
The Strand, Rye, Sussex TN31 7DB
Tel: 01797 222233

Real Ales, Bar Food, Restaurant Menu,
Accommodation, No Smoking Area, Disabled Facilities

50 Standard Inn
High Street, Rye, Sussex TN31 7EN
Tel: 01797 223393

Real Ales, Bar Food, Accommodation,
No Smoking Area

51 Star Inn
Church Street, Old Heathfield, Heathfield,
Sussex TN21 9AH
Tel: 01435 863570

Real Ales, Bar Food, Restaurant Menu,
No Smoking Area, Disabled Facilities

52 Three Cups Inn
Punnetts Town, Heathfield, Sussex TN21 9LR
Tel: 01435 830252

Real Ales, Bar Food, Restaurant Menu,
No Smoking Area, Disabled Facilities

53 Top O'the Hill
Rye Hill, Rye, Sussex TN31 7NH
Tel: 01797 223284

Real Ales, Restaurant Menu, Accommodation,
No Smoking Area, Disabled Facilities

54 Union Inn
East Street, Rye, Sussex TN31 7YJ
Tel: 01797 222334

Real Ales, Bar Food, Restaurant Menu,
No Smoking Area

55 The Wheel Inn

Heathfield Road, Burwash Weald,
East Sussex TN19 7LA

☎ 01435 882758 ⊕ www.thewheel.co.uk

Real Ales, Bar Food, Restaurant Menu, No Smoking
Area, Disabled Facilities

🍺 The pub is on the A265 Hurst Green-
    Heathfield road 2 miles west of Burwash

🐦 Harveys Sussex Best

🍴 12-2.30 & 6-9.30 (Sun 12-6, carvery 12-3)

🎵 Live music monthly, quiz fortnightly

🏕 Garden, car park

🚲 Major cards except Amex

🕐 11-11 (Sun 12-10.30)

🏛 Batemans (NT) 1 mile, Heathfield 4 miles,
    Hurst Green 5 miles

On the southern edge of the East Sussex High Weald, the **Wheel Inn** was built in about 1760 on a site occupied by an inn since the 13th century. The bar area has plenty of period appeal, with horns and brasses adorning original beams and plenty of stools, chairs and tables for relaxing with a drink or a meal. Harveys Sussex Best is the regular brew, with frequently changing guest ales including Summer Lightning and Shepherd Neame's Spitfire. Food is major part of the Wheel's business, with options covering everything from snacks and light bites to three-course meals. The home-made pies – steak, ale & mushroom; chicken, ham & mushroom – are real winners, and other favourites include fish specials and scrumptious desserts such as banoffee pie and sticky toffee pudding. The pub is fully accessible to wheelchair-users.

---

55 The Wheel Inn

Heathfield Road, Burwash Weald, Sussex TN19 7LA
Tel: 01435 882758

Real Ales, Bar Food, Restaurant Menu,
No Smoking Area, Disabled Facilities

See panel above

56 The White Dog Inn

Ewhurst Green, Robertsbridge, Sussex TN32 5TD
Tel: 01580 830264

Real Ales, Bar Food, Restaurant Menu,
No Smoking Area, Disabled Facilities

57 The White Hart

Cripps Corner Road, Robertsbridge,
Sussex TN32 5QS
Tel: 01580 830246

Real Ales, Bar Food, Restaurant Menu,
No Smoking Area, Disabled Facilities

58 The White Hart

High Street, Wadhurst, Sussex TN5 6AP
Tel: 01892 782878

Real Ales, Bar Food, No Smoking Area,
Disabled Facilities

59 White Vine House

24 High Street, Rye, Sussex TN31 7JF
Tel: 01797 224748

Restaurant Menu, Accommodation,
No Smoking Area

60 Ypres Castle Inn

Gun Garden, Rye, Sussex TN31 7HH
Tel: 01797 223248

Real Ales, Bar Food, Restaurant Menu, No Smoking
Area

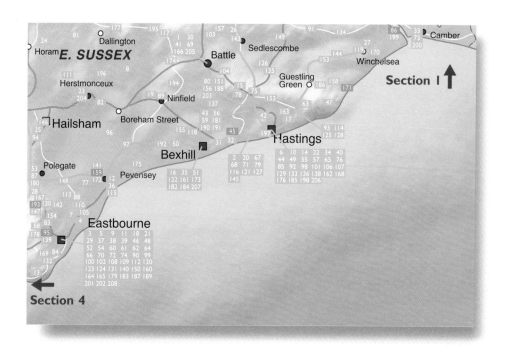

II   Pub or Inn Reference Number - Detailed Information

I2   Pub or Inn Reference Number - Summary Entry

⬤ ◼   Place of interest mentioned in the chapter introduction

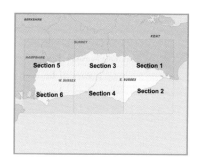

THE EAST SUSSEX COAST – EASTBOURNE TO WINCHELSEA

This stretch of the coast is linked with invaders: the Roman legions landed at Pevensey, as did William, Duke of Normandy, before defeating King Harold at the Battle of Hastings. The towns of Hastings and Battle have many museums and exhibitions telling the story of the momentous events of 1066. Other important centres in this area include the stylish resort of Eastbourne, with a range of visitor attractions including a classic pier and several museums and galleries. Close by is Beachy Head, one of the best-known coastal features in the whole country.

Battle

The site of the momentous Battle of Hastings in 1066, between the armies of Harold, Saxon king of England, and William, Duke of Normandy. After his victory, William fulfilled his vow of building an abbey on the very spot where Harold fell.

Bexhill-on-Sea

This small seaside resort was developed in the 1880s by the influential De La Warr family, whose name is carried by the **De La Warr Pavilion**, a 1930s building that is a renowned centre for arts and culture. The **Bexhill Festival of Motoring** takes place each year in May.

Camber

Camber Castle is a fine example of the coastal defences built by Henry VIII. It seems rather far inland today, but when it was built it held a commanding position on a spit of land on one side of the Rother estuary.

Eastbourne

This stylish seaside resort has a long list of visitor attractions, from the classic pier to a Martello Tower (now home to the **Puppet Museum**), the **Towner Art Gallery and Museum**, the **Museum of Shops**, the **RNLI Lifeboat Museum** and the **Military Museum of Sussex** in the Redoubt Fortress. Nearby **Beachy Head** is one of the most spectacular chalk cliffs in England, with a sheer drop of over 500 feet in places.

Hastings

Following the Battle of Hastings (which took place six miles away at Battle), the Normans began to build their first stone castle in England. Only ruins remain, but in a medieval siege tent the events of October

Beachy Head

1066 are told at the **1066 Story at Hastings Castle**. Attractions in town include the **Fishermen's Museum**, the **Shipwreck Heritage Centre** and two cliff railways.

Herstmonceux

Herstmonceux Castle, completed in 1440, was one of the first large-scale brick constructions in the country. In 1948, the Royal Observatory moved here from Greenwich, and although it has since moved again, the Castle now houses the **Herstmonceux Science Centre**.

Ninfield

To the north of the village stands redbrick **Ashburnham Place** in Ashburnham Park, which has survived much as it was conceived and laid out by Capability Brown in the 18th century.

Pevensey

Pevensey was the landing place for invading Roman forces and for William the Conqueror. William's half-brother Robert built **Pevensey Castle**, which today is run by English Heritage.

Polegate

Chief attraction here is **Polegate Windmill**, a splendid tower mill built in 1817. All the machinery is still in working order, and there's a small museum of milling on the site.

Sedlescombe

A pretty village stretched out along a sloping green where the parish pump still stands. To the southeast is the internationally renowned **Pestalozzi Children's Village**, founded by the Swiss educational reformer Johann Heinrich Pestalozzi to house children from Europe displaced during the Second World War.

Herstmonceux Castle

1 The 1066

11 High Street, Battle, Sussex TN33 0AE
Tel: 01424 773224

Real Ales, Bar Food, Restaurant Menu,
No Smoking Area

2 Admiral Benbow Inn

2 London Road , St Leonards-On-Sea,
Sussex TN37 6AE
Tel: 01424 421634

Disabled Facilities

3 The Albany

Grand Parade, Eastbourne, Sussex BN21 4DJ
Tel: 01323 722788

Restaurant Menu, Accommodation, No Smoking Area

4 The Alexandra Arms

453 Seaside, Eastbourne, Sussex BN22 7SA
Tel: 01323 720913

Real Ales, Bar Food, Restaurant Menu,
No Smoking Area

5 Alexandra Hotel

King Edwards Parade, Eastbourne,
Sussex BN21 4DR
Tel: 01323 720131

Accommodation, No Smoking Area

6 The Anchor

13 George Street, Hastings, Sussex TN34 3EG
Tel: 01424 424379

Real Ales, Bar Food, Disabled Facilities

7 Arlington Arms

360 Seaside, Eastbourne, Sussex BN22 7RY
Tel: 01323 724365

Real Ales, Bar Food, Restaurant Menu,
No Smoking Area, Disabled Facilities

8 The Ash Tree Inn

Brown Bread Street, Ashburnham, Battle,
Sussex TN33 9NX
Tel: 01424 892104

Real Ales, Bar Food, Restaurant Menu

9 Bar Bn21

155 Terminus Road, Eastbourne,
Sussex BN21 3NU
Tel: 01323 433041

Bar Food, Restaurant Menu, No Smoking Area,
Disabled Facilities

10 Bar Mode

206 Queens Road, Hastings, Sussex TN34 1QP
Tel: 01424 423324

Bar Food

11 The Beach Pub

74 Beach Road, Eastbourne, Sussex BN22 7AB
Tel: 01323 644578

Bar Food

12 Beach Tavern

Sea Road, Pevensey, Sussex BN24 6EH
Tel: 01323 761372

Real Ales, Bar Food, Restaurant Menu,
No Smoking Area

13 The Beachy Head

Beachy Head Road, Beachy Head, Eastbourne,
Sussex BN20 7YA
Tel: 01323 728060

Real Ales, Bar Food, Restaurant Menu,
No Smoking Area, Disabled Facilities

14 The Beaconsfield

45 Hughenden Road, Hastings, Sussex TN34 3TG
Tel: 01424 433364

Real Ales, Bar Food

15 Beauport Park Hotel

Hastings Road, St Leonards-On-Sea,
Sussex TN38 8EA
Tel: 01424 851222

Bar Food, Restaurant Menu, Accommodation,
No Smoking Area, Disabled Facilities

16 The Bell Hotel

Church Street, Bexhill-On-Sea, Sussex TN40 2HE
Tel: 01424 219654

Real Ales

17 Belmont
68-70 Harold Rd, Hastings, East Sussex TN35 5NL
Tel: 01424 425926
Real Ales

18 Black Horse
220 Seaside, Eastbourne, Sussex BN22 7QU
Tel: 01323 723143
Disabled Facilities

19 Blacksmiths Inn
The Green, Ninfield, Battle, Sussex TN33 9JL
Tel: 01424 892462
Real Ales, Bar Food, Restaurant Menu,
No Smoking Area, Disabled Facilities

20 Bo-Peep Public House
25 Grosvenor Crescent, St. Leonards-On-Sea,
East Sussex TN38 0AA
Tel: 01424 427371
Real Ales, Restaurant Menu, No Smoking Area,
Disabled Facilities

21 The Bourne Inn
80-82 Pevensey Road, Eastbourne,
Sussex BN21 3HT
Tel: 01323 736840
Real Ales, Bar Food, No Smoking Area

22 Brass Monkey
18 Havelock Road, Hastings, Sussex TN34 1BP
Tel: 01424 442406
Bar Food, Disabled Facilities

23 Brewers Arms
Gardner Street, Herstmonceux, Sussex BN27 4LB
Tel: 01323 832226
Real Ales, Bar Food, Restaurant Menu,
No Smoking Area, Disabled Facilities

24 Brewers Arms
Vines Cross, Heathfield, Sussex TN21 9EN
Tel: 01435 812288
Real Ales, Bar Food, Restaurant Menu,
No Smoking Area, Disabled Facilities

25 Bricklayers Arms
1 Ersham Road, Hailsham, Sussex BN27 3LA
Tel: 01323 841587
Real Ales

26 Brickwall Hotel
The Green, Sedlescombe, Battle,
Sussex TN33 0QA
Tel: 01424 870253
Restaurant Menu, Accommodation, No Smoking Area,
Disabled Facilities

27 The Bridge Inn
The Strand, Winchelsea, East Sussex TN36 4JT
Tel: 01797 224302
Real Ales, Bar Food, Restaurant Menu,
No Smoking Area, Disabled Facilities

28 The British Queen
The Triangle, Lower Willingdon, Eastbourne,
East Sussex BN20 9PG
Tel: 01323 484166
Real Ales, Restaurant Menu, No Smoking Area,
Disabled Facilities

29 Buccaneer
10 Compton Street, Eastbourne,
Sussex BN21 4BW
Tel: 01323 732829
Real Ales, Bar Food, Restaurant Menu,
No Smoking Area

30 Bull Inn
27 High Street, Battle, Sussex TN33 0EA
Tel: 01424 775171
Real Ales, Bar Food, Accommodation,
Disabled Facilities

31 Bull Inn
530 Bexhill Road, St. Leonards-On-Sea,
Sussex TN38 8AY
Tel: 01424 424984
Real Ales, Bar Food, Restaurant Menu,
No Smoking Area, Disabled Facilities

32 The Bulverhythe
311 Bexhill Road, St Leonards-On-Sea,
Sussex TN38 8AJ
Tel: 01424 420513
Disabled Facilities

33 Camber Castle
Lydd Road, Rye, Sussex TN31 7RJ
Tel: 01797 225429
Bar Food, No Smoking Area, Disabled Facilities

34 Carlisle
24 Pelham Street, Hastings, Sussex TN34 1PE
Tel: 01424 420193
Real Ales

35 The Castle
London Road, Bexhill-On-Sea, Sussex TN39 3JR
Tel: 01424 211730
Real Ales, Bar Food

36 The Castle Inn
72 Eastbourne Road, Pevensey,
Sussex BN24 6HS
Tel: 01323 764970
Real Ales, Bar Food, No Smoking Area

37 The Cavalier Inn
13-15 Carlisle Road, Eastbourne,
Sussex BN21 4BT
Tel: 01323 722307
Real Ales, Bar Food, Accommodation

38 Cavendish Hotel
Grand Parade, Eastbourne, Sussex BN21 4DH
Tel: 01323 410222
Bar Food, Restaurant Menu, Accommodation,
No Smoking Area, Disabled Facilities

39 Chatsworth Hotel
Grand Parade, Eastbourne, Sussex BN21 3YR
Tel: 01323 411016
Bar Food, Restaurant Menu, Accommodation,
No Smoking Area

40 The Chatsworth Hotel
Carlisle Parade, Hastings, Sussex TN34 1JG
Tel: 01424 720188
Bar Food, Restaurant Menu, Accommodation,
No Smoking Area, Disabled Facilities

41 Chequers Inn
Lower Lake, Battle, Sussex TN33 0AT
Tel: 01424 772088
Real Ales, Bar Food, Restaurant Menu,
Accommodation, No Smoking Area

42 Churchills Hotel
3 St Helens Crescent, Hastings, Sussex TN34 2EN
Tel: 01424 439359
Real Ales, Restaurant Menu, Accommodation,
No Smoking Area, Disabled Facilities

43 The Clarence
391 London Road, St Leonards-On-Sea,
Sussex TN37 6PH
Tel: 01424 422514
Bar Food

44 The Clown
9 Russell Street, Hastings, Sussex TN34 1QU
Tel: 01424 432267
Real Ales, Disabled Facilities

45 The Comet
Harley Shute Rd, St. Leonards-On-Sea,
East Sussex TN38 8BU
Tel: 01424 439117
Real Ales, Bar Food, No Smoking Area,
Disabled Facilities
See panel on page 16

46 Congress Hotels
31-41 Carlisle Road, Eastbourne, Sussex BN21 4JS
Tel: 01323 732118
Bar Food, Restaurant Menu, Accommodation,
No Smoking Area, Disabled Facilities

45 The Comet

Harley Shute, nr St Leonards-on-Sea,
East Sussex TN38 8BU
☎ 01424 439117

Real Ales, Bar Food, No Smoking Area, Disabled
Facilities

 From the A259 Bexhill-Hastings road turn left
(Bexhill) or right (Hastings) at Murco Garage
into Harley Shute Road. The inn is about 200
yards on the right.

🍺 Spitfire, Master Brew

🍴 12-2.30 & 6-8.30

🎵 Live music twice a month, quiz every second
Sunday, darts, pool

⛏ Garden, patio, car park

💳 Major cards accepted

🕐 12-11 (Sun to 10.30)

🏛 St Leonards 1 mile, Hastings 2 miles, Bexhill 2
miles

The **Comet** is a substantial redbrick in
built in 1952 and situated just off the
A259 west of St Leonards. Landlord Derick
Longley has an equally friendly greeting for
his regular customers and visitors to the
region, and in the comfortable bar a good
variety of Shepherd Neame and other
brews is served.

The food is mainly traditional, with home-
made pies, steaks, chicken dishes and curries,
and home-made sweets such as spotted dick,
apple crumble and chocolate fudge cake.

The inn hosts live music evenings twice a
month and a quiz every other Sunday. The
Comet also fields its own football team, with
Derick an enthusiastic player. At the front is a
little lawned garden with flowers and a wishing
well, while at the back a decking patio leads to
a large garden.

47 The Cove Continental

53 Waites Lane, Hastings, Sussex TN35 4AX
Tel: 01424 812110

Real Ales, Bar Food, Restaurant Menu,
No Smoking Area, Disabled Facilities

48 The Cumberland Hotel

34 - 36 Grand Parade, Eastbourne,
Sussex BN21 3YT
Tel: 01323 730342

Bar Food, Restaurant Menu, Accommodation, No
Smoking Area, Disabled Facilities

49 The Cutter

11-13 East Parade, Hastings, Sussex TN34 3AL
Tel: 01424 423449

50 The Denbigh

Little Common Road, Bexhill-On-Sea,
Sussex TN39 4JE
Tel: 01424 843817

Real Ales, Bar Food, Restaurant Menu,
No Smoking Area, Disabled Facilities

51 The Devonshire Arms

Devonshire Road, Bexhill-On-Sea, Sussex TN40 1AB
Tel: 01424 219413

Real Ales, Bar Food, No Smoking Area,
Disabled Facilities

52 The Dewdrop Inn

37-39 South Street, Eastbourne,
Sussex BN21 4UP
Tel: 01323 723313

Real Ales, Bar Food, No Smoking Area

53 The Dinkum
54 High Street, Polegate, Sussex BN26 6AG
Tel: 01323 482029
Real Ales, Bar Food, Restaurant Menu,
Disabled Facilities

54 The Dolphin
14 South Street, Eastbourne, Sussex BN21 4XF
Tel: 01323 723788
Real Ales, Disabled Facilities

55 Dolphin Inn
11-12 Rock-A-Nore Road, Hastings,
Sussex TN34 3DW
Tel: 01424 431197
Real Ales, Bar Food

56 Dripping Spring
34 Tower Road, St Leonards-On-Sea,
Sussex TN37 6JE
Tel: 01424 434055
Real Ales, Bar Food

57 Dripping Well
1 Dorset Place, Hastings, Sussex TN34 1LG
Tel: 01424 421686
Real Ales

58 The Drive
153 Victoria Drive, Eastbourne, Sussex BN20 8NH
Tel: 01323 729291
Real Ales, Bar Food, No Smoking Area,
Disabled Facilities

59 Duke
48 Duke Road, Silverhill, St Leonards-On-Sea,
Sussex TN37 7DN
Tel: 01424 436241
Real Ales

60 The Eagle
57 South Street, Eastbourne, Sussex BN21 4UT
Tel: 01323 722640
Real Ales, Bar Food

61 Elm Park Hotel
20 Cavendish Place, Eastbourne, Sussex BN21 3EJ
Tel: 01323 411511
Real Ales, Bar Food, Accommodation,
No Smoking Area, Disabled Facilities

62 Fairlands Hotel
15 Lascelles Terrace, Eastbourne,
East Sussex BN21 4BJ
Tel: 01323 733287
Restaurant Menu, Accommodation

63 Fairlight Lodge Hotel
Martineau Lane, Hastings, Sussex TN35 5DR
Tel: 01424 812104
Real Ales, Bar Food, Restaurant Menu,
Accommodation, No Smoking Area, Disabled Facilities

64 Farrars Hotel
8 Wilmington Gardens, Eastbourne,
Sussex BN21 4JN
Tel: 01323 723737
Bar Food, Restaurant Menu, Accommodation,
No Smoking Area, Disabled Facilities

65 First In Last Out Brewery
14-15 High Street, Hastings, Sussex TN34 3EY
Tel: 01424 425079
Real Ales, Bar Food, No Smoking Area,
Disabled Facilities

66 Flava Bar & Restaurant
32-34 Terminus Rd, Eastbourne,
East Sussex BN21 3LP
Tel: 01323 748844
Bar Food, Restaurant Menu, No Smoking Area,
Disabled Facilities

67 The Fountain Inn
26 Caves Road, St Leonards-On-Sea,
Sussex TN38 0BY
Tel: 01424 424095
Real Ales

68 The Fox Freehouse
31 32 North Street, St Leonards-On-Sea,
Sussex TN38 0EX
Tel: 01424 461800
Real Ales

69 George Hotel
23 High Street, Battle, Sussex TN33 0EA
Tel: 01424 775512
Bar Food, Restaurant Menu, Accommodation,
No Smoking Area, Disabled Facilities

70 The Gilderedge
11 Terminus Road, Eastbourne, Sussex BN21 3QL
Tel: 01323 732482
Real Ales, Bar Food, Restaurant Menu

71 Grand Hotel
Grand Parade, Hastings, Sussex TN38 0DD
Tel: 01424 428510
Bar Food, Restaurant Menu, Accommodation,
No Smoking Area, Disabled Facilities

72 Grand Hotel
King Edwards Parade, Eastbourne,
Sussex BN21 4EQ
Tel: 01323 412345
Real Ales, Bar Food, Restaurant Menu,
Accommodation, No Smoking Area, Disabled Facilities

73 The Green Owl Hotel
11 Old Lydd Rd, Camber, Rye, East
Sussex TN31 7RE
Tel: 01797 225284
Real Ales, Bar Food, Restaurant Menu,
Accommodation, No Smoking Area

74 Greenhouse
10 Station St, Eastbourne,
East Sussex BN21 4RG
Tel: 01323 738228
Real Ales, Bar Food, Restaurant Menu

75 Harrow Inn
828 The Ridge, St. Leonards-On-Sea,
Sussex TN37 7PX
Tel: 01424 751109
Real Ales, Bar Food, Restaurant Menu,
No Smoking Area, Disabled Facilities

76 The Hastings Arms
1-2 George Street, Hastings, Sussex TN34 3EG
Tel: 01424 722208
Real Ales, Bar Food, No Smoking Area,
Disabled Facilities

77 The Heron
27 High Street, Westham, Pevensey,
Sussex BN24 5LR
Tel: 01323 761041
Real Ales

78 High Beech
Battle Road, Hastings, Sussex TN37 7BS
Tel: 01424 851383
Real Ales, Bar Food, Restaurant Menu,
Accommodation, No Smoking Area, Disabled Facilities

79 Highland Inn
Boscobel Road, St Leonards-On-Sea,
Sussex TN38 0LU
Tel: 01424 420299
Real Ales, Bar Food, Restaurant Menu,
Accommodation, No Smoking Area, Disabled Facilities

80 Hollington Oak Public House
Wishing Tree Road, St. Leonards-On-Sea,
Sussex TN38 9LB
Tel: 01424 852495
Real Ales, Bar Food, Restaurant Menu,
No Smoking Area, Disabled Facilities

81 Horse & Groom

Rushlake Green, Heathfield, Sussex TN21 9QE
Tel: 01435 830320

Real Ales, Restaurant Menu, No Smoking Area

82 Horseshoe Inn

Posey Green, Windmill Hill, Hailsham,
East Sussex BN27 4RU
Tel: 01323 833265

Real Ales, Bar Food, Restaurant Menu,
Accommodation, No Smoking Area, Disabled Facilities

83 Hurst Arms

76 Willingdon Road, Eastbourne,
Sussex BN21 1TW
Tel: 01323 721762

Real Ales

84 Hydro Hotel

Mount Road, Eastbourne, Sussex BN20 7HZ
Tel: 01323 720643

Real Ales, Bar Food, Restaurant Menu,
Accommodation, No Smoking Area, Disabled Facilities

85 The Imperial

119 Queens Road, Hastings, Sussex TN34 1RL
Tel: 01424 435465

Real Ales, Bar Food, No Smoking Area

86 The Inkerman Arms

Rye Harbour Road, Rye, Sussex TN31 7TQ
Tel: 01797 222464

Real Ales, Bar Food, Restaurant Menu,
No Smoking Area, Disabled Facilities

See panel below

87 The Junction Tavern

99 Station Road, Polegate, Sussex BN26 6EB
Tel: 01323 482010

Real Ales, Bar Food, Restaurant Menu,
No Smoking Area, Disabled Facilities

88 The Kingfisher Tavern

Langley Shopping Centre, 64 Kingfisher Drive,
Eastbourne, Sussex BN23 7RT
Tel: 01323 765004

Real Ales, No Smoking Area, Disabled Facilities

---

86 The Inkerman Arms

Rye Harbour Road, Rye, East Sussex TN31 7TQ
☎ 01797 222464

Real Ales, Bar Food, Restaurant Menu, No Smoking Area, Disabled Facilities

- ☛ On A259 out of Rye centre take the first left signed Rye Harbour
- 🍺 Harveys, Greene King IPA, guests
- 🍴 12-2.30 & 7-9.15
- 🎵 Live music Saturday
- ⚓ Garden, boules pitch, car park
- 💳 Major cards except Amex
- 🕐 12-3 & 7-11 (closed Monday)
- 🏛 Rye 2 miles, Rye Nature Reserve 5 mins walk

Two cottages built in the 1800s were converted into a small, friendly inn situated at Rye Harbour, a short walk from Rye Nature Reserve. Marlene and Ken guarantee the warmest of welcomes at the Inkerman Arms, and the cosy little bar is well stocked with real ales, lagers, wines and spirits. In the bar or dining area visitors can enjoy a wide range of snacks and more substantial dishes – fresh fish is a speciality, and a particular favourite is cod cooked in a batter made to a special recipe. Other popular orders include steak, mushroom & ale pie, lasagne and chicken tikka masala.

On the social side, the inn hosts live music sessions on Saturdays and fields boules and cribbage teams in local leagues. There's a boules pitch in the garden.

89 The Kings Arms

Bexhill Road, Ninfield, Battle, Sussex TN33 9JB
Tel: 01424 892263

Real Ales, Bar Food, Restaurant Menu,
No Smoking Area, Disabled Facilities

90 The Kings Arms

222 Seaside, Eastbourne, East Sussex BN22 7QX
Tel: 01323 722274

Real Ales, Disabled Facilities

91 Kings Head

Rye Road, Udimore, Rye, Sussex TN31 6BG
Tel: 01424 882349

Real Ales, Bar Food, No Smoking Area

92 The Kings Head

25 Courthouse Street, Hastings,
Sussex TN34 3AU
Tel: 01424 439292

Real Ales

93 The Kings Head

61 Rye Road, Hastings, Sussex TN35 5DH
Tel: 01424 423767

Real Ales

94 The Kings Head

South Road, Hailsham, Sussex BN27 3NJ
Tel: 01323 843880

Real Ales, Disabled Facilities

95 The Lamb

36 High Street, Old Town, Eastbourne,
Sussex BN21 1HH
Tel: 01323 720545

Real Ales, Bar Food, Restaurant Menu,
No Smoking Area, Disabled Facilities

See panel below

95 The Lamb

High Street, Old Town, Eastbourne,
East Sussex BN21 1HH
☎ 01323 720545

Real Ales, Bar Food, Restaurant Menu, No Smoking
Area, Disabled Facilities

- In the main street of Old Town on the northern outskirts of Eastbourne
- Harveys
- 12-2.15 (Sun to 3.15) & 5.30-9 (Sun 7-9)
- Folk Club 1st and 3rd Wed of month
- Car park
- Major cards accepted
- 10.30am – 11pm (Sun 12-10.30)
- All the attractions of Eastbourne a short drive away

In the main street of Old Town, on the northern edge of Eastbourne, The Lamb has been in the excellent care of tenants Steve and Helen since 1990. Stepping into this eyecatching inn is like taking a walk back in time: the oldest part dates back to the 12th century, the main building to the 16th, and the décor and furnishings throughout have an irresistible old-world charm. The full range of the owning brewery – Harveys of Lewes – is on tap, and unpretentious home-cooked dishes are served every lunchtime and evening. The steak & ale pie is a great favourite, but everything's good and tasty, and for lighter appetites smaller snacks are serve all day. Steve and Helen have the invaluable assistance of an outstanding team at this splendid inn, guaranteeing that every visit is a real pleasure.

96 Lamb Inn
Wartling, Hailsham, Sussex BN27 IRY
Tel: 01323 832116
Real Ales, Bar Food, Restaurant Menu,
No Smoking Area

97 The Lamb Inn
Hooe, Battle, Sussex TN33 9HH
Tel: 01424 847891
Real Ales, Bar Food, Restaurant Menu,
No Smoking Area, Disabled Facilities

98 The Langham
16 Elphinstone Road, Hastings, Sussex TN34 2EQ
Tel: 01424 420858

99 Langham Hotel
43-49 Royal Parade, Eastbourne,
Sussex BN22 7AH
Tel: 01323 731451
Bar Food, Restaurant Menu, Accommodation,
No Smoking Area, Disabled Facilities

100 Lansdowne Hotel
King Edwards Parade, Eastbourne,
Sussex BN21 4EE
Tel: 01323 725174
Bar Food, Restaurant Menu, Accommodation,
No Smoking Area, Disabled Facilities

101 The Lansdowne Hotel
1-2 Robertson Terrace, Hastings, Sussex TN34 IJE
Tel: 01424 429605
Bar Food, Restaurant Menu, Accommodation,
No Smoking Area

102 The Lathom Hotel
4-6 Howard Square, Eastbourne,
Sussex BN21 4BG
Tel: 01323 641986
Restaurant Menu, Accommodation, No Smoking Area

103 Leeford Place Hotel
Whatlington Road, Whatlington, Battle,
Sussex TN33 0ND
Tel: 01424 772863
Real Ales, Bar Food, Restaurant Menu,
Accommodation, No Smoking Area, Disabled Facilities

104 Little Hemmingfold Hotel
Hastings Road, Battle, Sussex TN33 0TT
Tel: 01424 774338
Restaurant Menu, Accommodation, No Smoking Area

105 The Lodge
559 Seaside, Eastbourne, Sussex BN23 6NH
Tel: 01323 648133
Real Ales, Bar Food, Restaurant Menu,
No Smoking Area, Disabled Facilities

106 Lord Nelson
East Bourne Street, Hastings, Sussex TN34 3DP
Tel: 01424 423280
Real Ales

107 The Lord Warden
Manor Road, Hastings, Sussex TN34 3LP
Tel: 01424 420055
Real Ales

108 Mansion Hotel
Grand Parade, Eastbourne, Sussex BN21 3YS
Tel: 01323 727411
Real Ales, Bar Food, Accommodation,
No Smoking Area

109 The Marine
61 Seaside, Eastbourne, Sussex BN22 7NE
Tel: 01323 720464
Real Ales, Bar Food, Restaurant Menu,
No Smoking Area

110 The Martello Inn
Langney Rise, Eastbourne,
East Sussex BN23 7DD
Tel: 01323 766099
Real Ales, No Smoking Area, Disabled Facilities

111 The Merry Harriers
Cow Beech, Hailsham, Sussex BN27 4JQ
Tel: 01323 833108
Real Ales, Bar Food, Restaurant Menu,
No Smoking Area, Disabled Facilities

112 Merryfield Hotel
51 Royal Parade, Eastbourne, Sussex BN22 7AQ
Tel: 01323 723696
Accommodation

113 The Mill
Willingdon Drive, Eastbourne, Sussex BN23 8AL
Tel: 01323 460809
Bar Food, Restaurant Menu, No Smoking Area,
Disabled Facilities

114 Millars Arms
38 Winchelsea Road, Hastings, Sussex TN35 4JU
Tel: 01424 439075
Real Ales

115 Moorings
Seaville Drive, Pevensey, Sussex BN24 6AL
Tel: 01323 761126
Real Ales, Bar Food, No Smoking Area,
Disabled Facilities

116 The Nags Head
8-9 Gensing Road, St Leonards-On-Sea,
Sussex TN38 0ER
Tel: 01424 445973
Real Ales

117 Netherfield Arms
Netherfield Road, Netherfield, Battle,
Sussex TN33 9QD
Tel: 01424 838282
Real Ales, Bar Food, Restaurant Menu,
No Smoking Area

118 New Inn
Ninfield Road, Bexhill-On-Sea, Sussex TN39 5AE
Tel: 01424 210581
Real Ales

119 The New Inn
German Street, Winchelsea, Sussex TN36 4EN
Tel: 01797 226252
Real Ales, Bar Food, Restaurant Menu,
Accommodation, No Smoking Area, Disabled Facilities

120 New Wilmington Hotel
25-27 Compton Street, Eastbourne,
Sussex BN21 4DU
Tel: 01323 721219
Restaurant Menu, Accommodation, No Smoking Area

121 The Norman Arms
Norman Rd, St. Leonards-On-Sea, East
Sussex TN37 6NH
Tel: 01424 420827
Real Ales

122 Northern Hotel
72 Sea Road, Bexhill-On-Sea, Sussex TN40 1JL
Tel: 01424 212836
Bar Food, Restaurant Menu, Accommodation,
No Smoking Area, Disabled Facilities

123 The Nut House
96 Seaside Rd, Eastbourne, East Sussex BN21 3PF
Tel: 01323 648894
Real Ales, Bar Food

124 The Ocean Wave
29 Latimer Road, Eastbourne, Sussex BN22 7BZ
Tel: 01323 416459
Real Ales, Bar Food, Restaurant Menu,
Accommodation, No Smoking Area

125 Oddfellows Arms
Old London Road, Hastings, Sussex TN35 5BH
Tel: 01424 423242
Real Ales, Disabled Facilities

126 The Old Courthouse
Main Road, Hastings, Sussex TN35 4QE
Tel: 01424 751603
Real Ales, Bar Food, No Smoking Area

127 Old England
45 London Road , St Leonards-On-Sea,
Sussex TN37 6AJ
Tel: 01424 722154
Accommodation, Disabled Facilities

128 Old King John

39-41 Middle Road, Hastings, Sussex TN35 5DL
Tel: 01424 443310

Real Ales

129 The Palace Bars

White Rock Court, Hastings, Sussex TN34 1JP
Tel: 01424 439444

Real Ales, Bar Food, Restaurant Menu,
Disabled Facilities

130 The Parkfield

Lindfield Road, Eastbourne, Sussex BN22 0AU
Tel: 01323 502807

Real Ales, Disabled Facilities

131 Pier Hotel

4 Grand Parade, Eastbourne, Sussex BN21 3EH
Tel: 01323 649544

Bar Food, Restaurant Menu, Accommodation,
No Smoking Area, Disabled Facilities

132 Pilot Inn

89 Meads Street, Eastbourne, Sussex BN20 7RW
Tel: 01323 723440

Real Ales, Bar Food, Restaurant Menu,
No Smoking Area, Disabled Facilities

133 Pisaro's

10 South Terrace, Hastings, Sussex TN34 1SA
Tel: 01424 421363

Real Ales, Bar Food, Restaurant Menu,
No Smoking Area

134 The Plough

Cock Marling, Udimore, Rye,
East Sussex TN31 6AL
Tel: 01797 223381

Real Ales, Bar Food, No Smoking Area

135 Plough Inn

Moor Lane, Hastings, Sussex TN35 4QR
Tel: 01424 751066

Real Ales, Bar Food, Restaurant Menu,
No Smoking Area, Disabled Facilities

136 The Plough Inn

49 Priory Road, Hastings, Sussex TN34 3JJ
Tel: 01424 717832

Real Ales

137 The Plough Inn

Crowhurst, Battle, Sussex TN33 9AW
Tel: 01424 830310

Real Ales, Bar Food, Restaurant Menu,
No Smoking Area

138 Prince Albert

28 Cornwallis Street, Hastings, Sussex TN34 1SS
Tel: 01424 425481

Real Ales

139 The Prince Albert

9 High Street, Eastbourne, Sussex BN21 1HG
Tel: 01323 727754

Real Ales, Bar Food, Restaurant Menu

140 Princes Hotel

12-20 Lascelles Terrace, Eastbourne,
Sussex BN21 4BL
Tel: 01323 722056

Bar Food, Restaurant Menu, Accommodation,
Disabled Facilities

141 Priory Court Hotel

Castle Road, Pevensey, Sussex BN24 5LG
Tel: 01323 763150

Real Ales, Bar Food, Restaurant Menu,
Accommodation, No Smoking Area, Disabled Facilities

142 The Pubb

Mountfield Road, Eastbourne, Sussex BN22 9BS
Tel: 01323 503310

Real Ales, Disabled Facilities

143 Queens Head

The Green Avenue, Sedlescombe, Battle,
Sussex TN33 0QA
Tel: 01424 870228

Real Ales, Bar Food, Restaurant Menu,
No Smoking Area, Disabled Facilities

144 Queens Head

Parsonage Lane, Icklesham, Winchelsea,
Sussex TN36 4BL
Tel: 01424 814552

Real Ales, Bar Food, No Smoking Area

145 The Railway

1 Kings Road, St Leonards-On-Sea, Sussex TN37 6EA
Tel: 01424 461083

Real Ales

146 The Railway Tavern

17 Station Road, Hailsham, Sussex BN27 2BH
Tel: 01323 842442

Real Ales

147 Red Lion

99 Wish Hill, Willingdon, Eastbourne,
Sussex BN20 9HQ
Tel: 01323 502062

Real Ales, Bar Food, Restaurant Menu,
No Smoking Area, Disabled Facilities

148 The Red Lion

Lion Hill, Stone Cross, Pevensey, Sussex BN24 5EG
Tel: 01323 761468

Real Ales, Bar Food, Restaurant Menu,
No Smoking Area, Disabled Facilities

149 The Red Lion

Brede, Rye, East Sussex TN31 6EJ
Tel: 01424 882188

Real Ales, Bar Food, Restaurant Menu,
No Smoking Area

150 Regent Hotel

3 Cavendish Place, Eastbourne,
East Sussex BN21 3EJ
Tel: 01323 731258

Bar Food, Restaurant Menu, Accommodation,
No Smoking Area

151 The Rising Sun

173 Battle Road, St Leonards-On-Sea,
Sussex TN37 7AJ
Tel: 01424 427030

Real Ales, Disabled Facilities

152 Robert De Mortain

373 The Ridge, Hastings, Sussex TN34 2RD
Tel: 01424 751061

Real Ales, Bar Food, Restaurant Menu,
No Smoking Area, Disabled Facilities

153 Robin Hood Inn

Main Road, Icklesham, Winchelsea,
Sussex TN36 4BD
Tel: 01424 814277

Real Ales, Bar Food, Restaurant Menu,
No Smoking Area, Disabled Facilities

154 The Rodmill

Rangemore Drive, Eastbourne, Sussex BN21 2QP
Tel: 01323 731784

Real Ales, Bar Food, Restaurant Menu,
No Smoking Area, Disabled Facilities

155 Rose & Crown Hungry Horse

Turkey Road, Bexhill-On-Sea, Sussex TN39 5HH
Tel: 01424 214625

Real Ales, Bar Food, Restaurant Menu,
No Smoking Area, Disabled Facilities

156 The Royal Albert

293 Battle Road, St Leonards-On-Sea,
Sussex TN37 7AP
Tel: 01424 851066

No Smoking Area, Disabled Facilities

157 Royal Oak

Woodmans Green, Whatlington, Battle,
Sussex TN33 0NJ
Tel: 01424 870492

Real Ales, Bar Food, Restaurant Menu,
No Smoking Area

158 Royal Oak

Pett Road, Pett, Hastings, Sussex TN35 4HG
Tel: 01424 812515

Real Ales, Bar Food, Restaurant Menu,
No Smoking Area, Disabled Facilities

159 The Royal Oak & Castle

High Street, Pevensey, East Sussex BN24 5LE
☎ 01323 762371

🌐 www.royaloakandcastleinn.co.uk

Real Ales, Bar Food, Restaurant Menu,
Accommodation, No Smoking Area

☞ The pub is in the main street of Pevensey,
next to the Castle

🍺 Harveys Sussex Best

🍴 12-2 (Sun to 4) & 6-9 (Sun to 8.30)

🛏 3 en suite rooms

🎵 Regular live music evenings

🍴 Garden, side parking or NCP

💳 Major cards except Amex

🕐 11-11 (Sun 12-10.30)

🏛 Castle, 1066 Walk; Herstmonceux 3 miles,
Hailsham 5 miles, Eastbourne 5 miles

Next to the Castle in the heart of
Pevensey, the **Royal Oak & Castle Inn**
attracts visitors from near and far. With its fine
ales and wines, superb food, comfortable
bedrooms and convivial atmosphere, it's a
great place to pause for a drink or a snack, or
to linger over a meal in the bar, the colourful
restaurant or out in the garden. Typical dishes
include grilled sardines and deep-fried scampi
(both available as starter or main course), beef
burger with bacon, herbs and melted cheese,
smoked haddock and spring onion fishcakes or
a vegetarian option such as baked mushrooms
filled with a cheese and leek sauce. The inn is
also a pleasant spot for an overnight stay or
longer break in well-appointed bedrooms,
(two having en suite showers, the the other an
en suite bath and no shower). All have tranquil
views.

159 The Royal Oak & Castle

High Street, Pevensey, Sussex BN24 5LE
Tel: 01323 762371

Real Ales, Bar Food, Restaurant Menu,
Accommodation, No Smoking Area

See panel above

160 The Royal Sovereign

12 Seaside Road, Eastbourne, Sussex BN21 3PA
Tel: 01323 722310

Real Ales, Bar Food

161 The Royal Sovereign

15 Sea Road, Bexhill-On-Sea, Sussex TN40 1EE
Tel: 01424 213427

Real Ales

162 The Royal Standard

Hastings Wall East Street, Hastings,
Sussex TN34 3AP
Tel: 01424 420163

Real Ales, Bar Food, Restaurant Menu

163 Royal Sussex Arms

242 Old London Road, Hastings, Sussex TN35 5LT
Tel: 01424 432926

Real Ales, Disabled Facilities

164 Saffrons Hotel

30-32 Jevington Gardens, Eastbourne,
Sussex BN21 4HN
Tel: 01323 725539

Restaurant Menu, Accommodation, No Smoking Area

165 Sea Beach House Hotel

39-40 Marine Parade, Eastbourne,
Sussex BN22 7AY
Tel: 01323 410458

Restaurant Menu, Accommodation, No Smoking Area

166 The Senlac

Station Road, Battle, Sussex TN33 0DE
Tel: 01424 772034

Real Ales, Bar Food, Restaurant Menu,
No Smoking Area, Disabled Facilities

167 Seven Sisters

Seven Sisters Road, Eastbourne, Sussex BN22 0QT
Tel: 01323 502162

Real Ales, Bar Food, No Smoking Area,
Disabled Facilities

168 The Shah

144 Mount Pleasant Road, Hastings,
Sussex TN34 3SN
Tel: 01424 439062

Real Ales

169 The Ship

33-35 Meads Street, Eastbourne,
Sussex BN20 7RH
Tel: 01323 733815

Real Ales, Bar Food, Restaurant Menu,
No Smoking Area, Disabled Facilities

170 The Ship Inn

Sea Road, Winchelsea Beach, Winchelsea,
Sussex TN36 4LH
Tel: 01797 225521

Real Ales, Bar Food, Restaurant Menu,
No Smoking Area, Disabled Facilities

171 The Smuggler

Pett Level Road, Pett Level, nr Hastings,
East Sussex TN35 4EH
☎ 01424 813491

Real Ales, Bar Food, Restaurant Menu, Accommodation, No Smoking Area, Disabled Facilities

☛ 6 miles from Hastings off the road to
Winchelsea and Rye. The inn stands almost on
the beach

🍺 Harveys Best, London Pride, Sussex Pride

🍴 12-2 & 6-9 (Sun 12-3 only)

🎵 Live music weekends, darts, billiards

⛲ Garden, patio, car park

💳 Major cards except Amex

🕐 11-3 & 6-11, Sat 11-11, Sun 12-10.30

🏛 Hastings 6 miles, Rye 6 miles

Mike and Lynn Mercer, their family and staff
welcome visitors to the Smuggler, a
building of substance that dates from the
1930s and was originally a beach club. It stands
practically on the beach on the coast road that
runs from Hastings to Winchelsea and attracts
a strong following of local residents and
tourists enjoying the delights of the Sussex
towns, villages and coast. The resident ales are
joined by a monthly changing guest, and the
food (served every session except Sunday
evening) ranges from snacks to battered cod,
steak pie, steaks, chicken curry and the popular
Saturday evening and Sunday lunch carvery.
The smuggler depicted on the inn's sign looks
rather jolly, an indication that this is among the
most friendly and sociable of pubs. Picnic
benches are set out in the front garden, and
the terrace at the back overlooks the sea.

171 The Smuggler
Pett Level Road, Pett Level, Hastings,
Sussex TN35 4EH
Tel: 01424 813491
Real Ales, Bar Food, Restaurant Menu,
Accommodation, No Smoking Area, Disabled Facilities
See panel opposite

172 The Smugglers Inn
High Street, Pevensey, Sussex BN24 5LF
Tel: 01323 762112
Real Ales, Bar Food, Restaurant Menu,
Accommodation, No Smoking Area, Disabled Facilities

173 The Sportsman
15 Sackville Road, Bexhill-On-Sea, Sussex TN39 3JD
Tel: 01424 214214
Real Ales, Bar Food

174 Squirrel Inn
North Trade Road, Battle, Sussex TN33 9LJ
Tel: 01424 772717
Real Ales, Bar Food, Restaurant Menu,
No Smoking Area, Disabled Facilities

175 The Star Inn
Normans Bay, Pevensey, Sussex BN24 6QG
Tel: 01323 762648
Real Ales, Bar Food, Restaurant Menu,
No Smoking Area, Disabled Facilities

176 The Street
53 Robertson Street, Hastings, Sussex TN34 1HY
Tel: 01424 424458
Bar Food

177 The Swan Inn
Woods Corner, Dallington, Heathfield,
Sussex TN21 9LB
Tel: 01424 838242
Real Ales, Bar Food, Restaurant Menu,
No Smoking Area

178 The Tally Ho
42 Church Street, Eastbourne, Sussex BN21 1JB
Tel: 01323 732083
Real Ales, Bar Food, Restaurant Menu,
No Smoking Area, Disabled Facilities

179 Terminus Hotel
153 Terminus Road, Eastbourne,
Sussex BN21 3NU
Tel: 01323 733964
Real Ales, Bar Food, Restaurant Menu,
No Smoking Area, Disabled Facilities

180 The Thoroughbred
6A Grand Parade, Polegate, Sussex BN26 5HG
Tel: 01323 484023
Real Ales, Accommodation

181 Tower Pub
251 The Tower London Road Business Park,
St Leonards-On-Sea, Sussex TN37 6NB
Tel: 01424 721773
Real Ales

182 The Town Crier
23 London Road, Bexhill-On-Sea, Sussex TN39 3JR
Tel: 01424 215793

183 The Townhouse
6 Bolton Rd, Eastbourne, East Sussex BN21 3JX
Tel: 01323 734900
Bar Food, No Smoking Area

184 The Traffers Bar
19 Egerton Road, Bexhill-On-Sea,
Sussex TN39 3HJ
Tel: 01424 210240
Real Ales, Bar Food, Restaurant Menu,
No Smoking Area

185 The Tubman
57 Cambridge Road, Hastings, Sussex TN34 1EL
Tel: 01424 420074
Disabled Facilities

193 The Wheatsheaf

2 Church Street, Willingdon, nr Eastbourne,
East Sussex BN20 9HP
☎ 01323 502069

Real Ales, Bar Food, No Smoking Area

☞ On the A3270 between Eastbourne and Polegate

🍺 Harveys, London Pride, Courage

🍴 12-2 & 6.30-9 (no food Mon or Tues evenings)

🍺 Beer garden, car park

💳 Major cards accepted

🕐 11-3 & 5-11 (all day Sat & Sun)

🏛 Eastbourne 1 mile

The **Wheatsheaf** is located in Willingdon, just minutes up the A22 from Eastbourne – close enough for all that town's amenities and also well placed for travelling east or west with the A27 less than a mile away. Maxine and Stuart Wells took over this timber-fronted early 19th century pub in July 2005 and are already well on the way to making it once again the busy pub they knew as customers. A good choice of real ales is available in the immaculately kept bar, and the chef uses the best local suppliers for her varied dishes, freshly prepared and served lunchtime and evening from Monday-Sunday lunchtimes and Wednesday to Saturday evenings. The menu proposes a selection of traditional favourites such as whitebait, fish fried in a lager batter, lasagne, liver & bacon and steak & ale pie.

186 Two Sawyers

Pett Road, Hastings, Sussex TN35 4HB
Tel: 01424 812255

Real Ales, Bar Food, Restaurant Menu,
No Smoking Area, Disabled Facilities

187 Victoria Hotel

27 Latimer Rd, Eastbourne, East Sussex BN22 7BU
Tel: 01323 722673

Real Ales, Accommodation, Disabled Facilities

188 Victoria Inn

290 Battle Road, St Leonards-On-Sea,
Sussex TN37 7BA
Tel: 01424 851755

Real Ales, Bar Food, Restaurant Menu,
No Smoking Area

189 Waterfront Lodge

11-12 Roysal Parade, Eastbourne, Sussex BN21 3JU
Tel: 01323 646566

Real Ales, Bar Food, Accommodation,
No Smoking Area

190 The Welcome Stranger

55 Sediescombe Road North, St. Leonards-On-Sea,
Sussex TN37 7DA
Tel: 01424 423180

Real Ales, Bar Food, Restaurant Menu,
Accommodation

191 The Wheat Sheaf

172 Bohemia Rd, St. Leonards-On-Sea,
East Sussex TN37 6RP
Tel: 01424 432803

Real Ales, Disabled Facilities

192 The Wheatsheaf

2 Barnhorn Road, Little Common, Bexhill-On-Sea,
Sussex TN39 4LR
Tel: 01424 845963

Bar Food, Restaurant Menu, No Smoking Area,
Disabled Facilities

193 The Wheatsheaf
2 Church Street, Willingdon, Sussex BN20 9HP
Tel: 01323 502069

Real Ales, Bar Food, No Smoking Area

See panel opposite

194 The White Hart
The Green, Catsfield, Battle, Sussex TN33 9DJ
Tel: 01424 892650

Real Ales, Bar Food, Restaurant Menu,
No Smoking Area, Disabled Facilities

195 The White Hart Inn
Netherfield, Battle, East Sussex TN33 9QH
Tel: 01424 838382

Real Ales, Bar Food, Restaurant Menu,
No Smoking Area, Disabled Facilities

196 The White Horse Inn
Bodle Street Green, Hailsham, Sussex BN27 4RE
Tel: 01323 833243

Real Ales, Bar Food, Restaurant Menu,
No Smoking Area, Disabled Facilities

197 The White Rock Hotel
1-10 White Rock, Hastings, East Sussex TN34 1JU
Tel: 01424 422240

Real Ales, Bar Food, Accommodation,
No Smoking Area

198 The Whitefriars
127 Priory Road , Hastings, Sussex TN34 3JD
Tel: 01424 437745

Real Ales, Bar Food

199 William The Conqueror
Rye Harbour, Rye, Sussex TN31 7TU
Tel: 01797 223315

Real Ales, Bar Food, Disabled Facilities

200 Winchelsea Lodge
Hastings Road, Winchelsea, Sussex TN31 7RH
Tel: 01797 226211

Real Ales, Bar Food, Restaurant Menu,
Accommodation, No Smoking Area, Disabled Facilities

201 Windsor Tavern
165 Langney Road, Eastbourne, Sussex BN22 8AH
Tel: 01323 726206

Real Ales, Bar Food, Restaurant Menu,
No Smoking Area

202 Wish Tower Hotel
1-3 King Edwards Parade, Eastbourne,
Sussex BN21 4EB
Tel: 01323 722676

Bar Food, Restaurant Menu, Accommodation,
No Smoking Area, Disabled Facilities

203 Wishing Tree
Wishing Tree Road North, St Leonards-On-Sea,
Sussex TN38 9LJ
Tel: 01424 851473

Real Ales

204 The Woolpack
Gardner Street, Hailsham, Sussex BN27 4LE
Tel: 01323 833270

Real Ales, Bar Food

205 Ye Olde Kings Head
37 Mount Street, Battle, Sussex TN33 0EG
Tel: 01424 772317

Real Ales, Bar Food, Disabled Facilities

206 Ye Olde Pump House
64 George Street, Hastings, Sussex TN34 3EE
Tel: 01424 422016

Real Ales, Bar Food, Restaurant Menu,
Accommodation, No Smoking Area, Disabled Facilities

207 The York Hotel
92 London Road, Bexhill-On-Sea, Sussex TN39 3LE
Tel: 01424 224275

Real Ales, Bar Food, Restaurant Menu,
Accommodation, No Smoking Area

208 York House Hotel
14-22 Royal Parade, Eastbourne, Sussex BN22 7AP
Tel: 01323 412918

Bar Food, Restaurant Menu, Accommodation,
No Smoking Area, Disabled Facilities

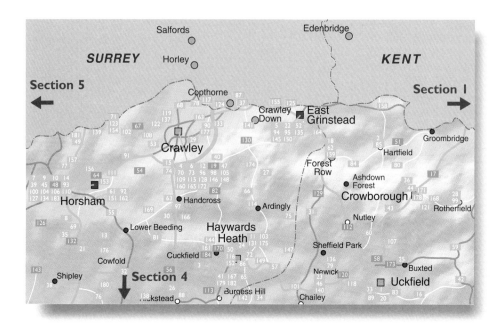

SURREY

KENT

Section 5

Section 1

Salfords

Edenbridge

Horley

Copthorne

Crawley Down

East Grinstead

Groombridge

Crawley

Hartfield

Forest Row

Ashdown Forest

Horsham

Handcross

Crowborough

Rotherfield

Ardingly

Nutley

Lower Beeding

Haywards Heath

Sheffield Park

Cowfold

Cuckfield

Buxted

Shipley

Section 4

Newick

Uckfield

Burgess Hill

Chailey

- **11** Pub or Inn Reference Number - Detailed Information
- **12** Pub or Inn Reference Number - Summary Entry
- ● ■ Place of interest mentioned in the chapter introduction

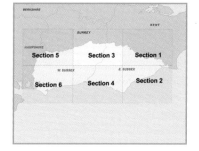

THE WEST SUSSEX WEALD

'Weald' means 'Forest', but although some wooded areas remain, most of the landscape is one of pastures enclosed by hedgerows. This part of Sussex, too, has a number of historic country houses, including the Victorian Standen near East Grinstead and Wakehurst Place, near Ardingly, where the collection of trees and shrubs is leased to the Royal Botanical Gardens at Kew. There are two other great gardens in this region – Leonardslee at Lower Beeding and Nymans at Handcross. The chief town of the region is Horsham.

Ardingly

The home of the showground for the South of England Agricultural Society. To the west, a tributary of the River Ouse has been dammed to form **Ardingly Reservoir**, a 200-acre lake that offers fishing, waterside walks and a nature trail. At the top of the reservoir, **Wakehurst Place** is run and maintained by the Royal Botanic Gardens, Kew. Top attractions include the Millennium Seed Bank, which aims to continue the survival of many thousands of plant species.

Ashdown Forest

This ancient tract of sandy heathland and woodland on the high ridges of the Weald is designated an Area of Outstanding Natural Beauty, a Site of Special Scientific Interest and a Special Protection Area for birds.

Buxted

The great house of **Buxted Park** was built along classical lines in 1725 and restored by architect Basil Ionides after a fire. Among its treasures are doors and chimney pieces by Robert Adam, and cabinets and pillars from grand London houses and country mansions.

Cuckfield

To the north of Cuckfield lie **Borde Hill Gardens**, a splendidly, typically English garden of special botanical interest set in 200 acres of spectacular parkland and woods.

Wakehurst Place, Ardingly

East Grinstead

East Grinstead has a long and interesting history that can be explored in the town museum. To the south lies **Standen**, a remarkable late-Victorian country mansion that's a showcase for the Arts & Crafts Movement. William Morris himself designed the internal furnishings. From a station near Standen runs the renowned **Bluebell Railway**, which offers a very pleasant journey by steam train through the Sussex Weald to Sheffield Park.

Groombridge

The superb manor house **Groombridge Place** contains a small museum dedicated to Sir Arthur Conan Doyle, a frequent visitor to the house.

Groombridge Place Gardens

Handcross

Close to this little village on the old London to Brighton road are two glorious gardens – **Nymans**, developed by the Messel family, and **High Beeches**, with a collection of rare and exotic plants as well as native wild flowers in a natural meadow setting.

Horsham

Horsham's architectural gem is **The Causeway**, a quiet tree-lined street that runs from the town hall to the 12th century Church of St Mary.

Lower Beeding

South of the village lie the beautiful **Leonardslee Gardens**, world famous for the spring displays of azaleas, magnolias and rhododendrons around seven landscaped lakes.

Sheffield Green

The village takes its name from the manor house remodelled in the 1770s by James Wyatt for the 1st Earl of Sheffield. At the same time as creating **Sheffield Park**, the Earl commissioned Capability Brown and Humphry Repton to landscape the gardens.

Shipley

Shipley was the home of Hilaire Belloc, who lived at King's Land from 1906 until his death in 1953. In his garden stands **Shipley Mill**, the only remaining working smock mill in Sussex. The composer John Ireland is buried in the 12th century village church.

1 Alma

Framfield Road, Uckfield, Sussex TN22 5AJ
Tel: 01825 762232

Real Ales, Bar Food, No Smoking Area,
Disabled Facilities

2 The Anchor Inn

Church Street, Hartfield, Sussex TN7 4AG
Tel: 01892 770424

Real Ales, Bar Food, Restaurant Menu,
Accommodation, No Smoking Area, Disabled Facilities

3 The Ansty Cross Inn

Cuckfield Road, Ansty, Haywards Heath,
Sussex RH17 5AG
Tel: 01444 413038

Real Ales, Bar Food, Restaurant Menu,
No Smoking Area

4 The Apple Tree

Ewhurst Road, Crawley, Sussex RH11 7HD
Tel: 01293 521907

Real Ales, Bar Food, Restaurant Menu

5 Bar Cuba

35 High Street, East Grinstead, Sussex RH19 3AF
Tel: 01342 327947

Real Ales, Bar Food, Restaurant Menu,
No Smoking Area

6 Bar Med

100 High St, Crawley, West Sussex RH10 1BZ
Tel: 01293 560802

No Smoking Area, Disabled Facilities

7 Bar Vin

3 Market Square, Horsham, Sussex RH12 1EU
Tel: 01403 250640

Real Ales, Bar Food, Restaurant Menu,
No Smoking Area, Disabled Facilities

8 Bax Castle Restaurant & Free House

Two Mile Ash, Southwater, Horsham,
Sussex RH13 0LA
Tel: 01403 730369

Real Ales, Bar Food, Restaurant Menu,
No Smoking Area

9 The Bear Inn

17 Market Square, Horsham, Sussex RH12 1EU
Tel: 01403 260700

Real Ales, Disabled Facilities

10 The Bedford

Station Road, Horsham, Sussex RH13 5EY
Tel: 01403 253128

Real Ales

11 The Bent Arms Hotel

98 High St, Lindfield, Haywards Heath,
West Sussex RH16 2HP
Tel: 01444 483146

Real Ales, Bar Food, Restaurant Menu,
Accommodation, No Smoking Area

12 The Black Dog

Barnfield Road, Crawley, Sussex RH10 8DS
Tel: 01293 526628

13 Black Horse

Nuthurst Street, Nuthurst, Horsham,
Sussex RH13 6LH
Tel: 01403 891272

Real Ales, Bar Food, Restaurant Menu,
No Smoking Area, Disabled Facilities

14 Black Jug

31 North Street, Horsham, Sussex RH12 1RJ
Tel: 01403 253526

Real Ales, Bar Food, Restaurant Menu,
No Smoking Area

15 The Black Swan

Old Brighton Rd, Crawley, West Sussex RI111 9AJ
Tel: 01293 612261

Real Ales, Bar Food, Restaurant Menu,
No Smoking Area, Disabled Facilities

16 Blackboys Inn

Lewes Road, Blackboys, Uckfield, Sussex TN22 5LG
Tel: 01825 890283

Real Ales, Bar Food, Restaurant Menu,
No Smoking Area

17 The Boar's Head Inn

Boarshead, Crowborough, Sussex TN6 3HD
Tel: 01892 652412

Real Ales, Bar Food, Restaurant Menu,
No Smoking Area

See panel below

18 Brambletye Hotel

The Square, Lewes Road, Forest Row,
Sussex RH18 5EZ
Tel: 01342 824144

Real Ales, Bar Food, Restaurant Menu,
Accommodation, No Smoking Area

19 The Brewery Shades

85 High Street, Crawley, Sussex RH10 1BA
Tel: 01293 514105

Real Ales, Bar Food, Restaurant Menu,
No Smoking Area

See panel opposite

20 The Brickmakers Arms

New Road, Uckfield, Sussex TN22 5TG
Tel: 01825 762795

Real Ales, Bar Food

21 Bridge House Inn

Copsale Road, Copsale, Horsham,
Sussex RH13 6QT
Tel: 01403 730383

Real Ales, Bar Food, Restaurant Menu,
No Smoking Area, Disabled Facilities

22 The Broadway

London Road Business Park, East Grinstead,
Sussex RH19 1EP
Tel: 01342 410306

Bar Food, Restaurant Menu, No Smoking Area,
Disabled Facilities

---

17 The Boar's Head Inn

Boarshead, nr Crowborough, East Sussex TN6 3HD
☎ 01892 652412

Real Ales, Bar Food, Restaurant Menu,
No Smoking Area

☛ From the A26 Tunbridge Wells-Crowborough road turn left at sign to North Boarshead. Turn right at T junction

🍺 Harveys, London Pride, Adnams

🍴 12-2 (7 days) & 7-9 (not Sun or Mon)

🛏 Self-catering accommodation planned for 2006

⚓ Beer garden, car park

💳 Major cards except Amex

🕐 11.30-2.30 (Sat to 3.30) & 6-11

🏛 Crowborough 2 miles, Wilderness Woods 2 miles

In a quiet setting off the Tunbridge Wells-Crowborough road, the **Boar's Head** is a very traditional English pub dating back to the 17th century. Behind the neat exterior, the old-world charm is epitomised by ancient black beams and a lovely inglenook hearth in the bar, where the civilised atmosphere (no machines) makes it a pleasure to enjoy good conversation with a glass of well-kept ale. Traditional pub dishes are served in the bar and in the restaurant, which overlooks an attractive beer garden. Plans for 2006 include the opening of self-catering accommodation, which will make the Boar's Head a splendid base for exploring the region. The many local attractions include Beacon House, sometime home of Sir Arthur Conan Doyle and Wilderness Woods, and Boarshead Golf Course is next to the pub.

19 The Brewery Shades

85 High Street, Crawley, West Sussex RH10 1BA
☎ 01293 514105

Real Ales, Bar Food, Restaurant Menu,
No Smoking Area

☛ Centrally located in Crawley, a short drive from the A23 and M23

🍺 Greene King IPA, Abbot Ale, 2 guests

🍴 10am-10pm

♪ Occasional entertainment and themed food evenings, usually on Wednesday

💳 Major cards except Amex and Diners

🕐 Open all day, every day

🏛 Friday and Saturday market close by, Gatwick Airport 4 miles

Situated close to the market square of Crawley, a stop on the old London to Brighton coaching route, the **Brewery Shades** has a long and interesting history that starts way back in the 15th century. Later a gaol and a working brewery, this pub has retained its historical charm and is open all day, seven days a week, both for drinks – four real ales always on tap – and for hot and cold food, served in the traditional bar or in the comfortable dining area.

23 The Bull Inn

The Green, Newick, Lewes, Sussex BN8 4LA
Tel: 01825 722055

Real Ales, Bar Food, Restaurant Menu,
Accommodation, No Smoking Area, Disabled Facilities

24 Burrell Arms

Commercial Square, Haywards Heath,
Sussex RH16 1EA
Tel: 01444 453214

Real Ales, Bar Food, No Smoking Area

25 The Buxted Inn

High Street, Buxted, Uckfield, Sussex TN22 4LA
Tel: 01825 733510

Real Ales, Bar Food, Restaurant Menu,
Accommodation, No Smoking Area, Disabled Facilities

26 Castle Inn & China Brasserie

London Road Business Park, Haywards Heath,
Sussex RH17 5LZ
Tel: 01444 881223

Bar Food, Restaurant Menu, Disabled Facilities

27 Cat Inn

Queen's Square, West Hoathly, East Grinstead,
West Sussex RH19 4PP
Tel: 01342 810369

Real Ales, Bar Food, Restaurant Menu,
No Smoking Area

28 Catts Inn

High Street, Rotherfield, Crowborough,
Sussex TN6 3LH
Tel: 01892 852546

Real Ales, Bar Food, Disabled Facilities

29 Charcoal Burner

Weald Drive, Furnace Green, Crawley,
Sussex RH10 6NY
Tel: 01293 653981

Real Ales, Bar Food

30 Chequers At Slaugham

Slaugham, Nr Handcross, Sussex RH17 6AQ
Tel: 01444 400239

Bar Food, Restaurant Menu, Accommodation,
No Smoking Area, Disabled Facilities

31 Coach & Horses

School Lane, Danehill, Haywards Heath,
Sussex RH17 7JF
Tel: 01825 740369

Real Ales, Bar Food, Restaurant Menu,
No Smoking Area, Disabled Facilities

32 The Coach House

Horsham Road, Horsham, Sussex RH13 8BT
Tel: 01403 864247

Real Ales, Bar Food, Restaurant Menu,
Accommodation, No Smoking Area, Disabled Facilities

33 The Cock & Bull

New Town, Uckfield, Sussex TN22 5DL
Tel: 01825 760999

Real Ales, Bar Food, Restaurant Menu,
No Smoking Area, Disabled Facilities

34 The Cock Inn

North Common Rd, Wivelsfield Green,
Haywards Heath, West Sussex RH17 7RH
Tel: 01444 471668

Real Ales, Bar Food, Restaurant Menu,
Accommodation, No Smoking Area, Disabled Facilities

35 The Cock Inn

Worthing Road, Southwater, Horsham,
Sussex RH13 9HG
Tel: 01403 730205

Real Ales, Bar Food, Disabled Facilities

36 The Coopers Arms

Coopers Lane, Crowborough, Sussex TN6 1SN
Tel: 01892 654796

Real Ales, Bar Food

37 The Copthorne
Effingham Park Hotel

West Park Road, Copthorne, Crawley,
Sussex RH10 3EU
Tel: 01342 714994

Real Ales, Bar Food, Restaurant Menu,
Accommodation, No Smoking Area, Disabled Facilities

38 The Countryman

Countryman Lane, Whitehall, Horsham,
Sussex RH13 8PZ
Tel: 01403 741383

Real Ales, Bar Food, Restaurant Menu,
No Smoking Area

39 The Coupe

Merryfield Drive, Horsham, Sussex RH12 2AA
Tel: 01403 254404

Real Ales, Disabled Facilities

40 Cowdray Arms

London Road, Balcombe, Sussex RH17 6QD
Tel: 01444 811280

Real Ales, Bar Food, Restaurant Menu,
No Smoking Area

41 The Cricketers

23 West Street, Burgess Hill, Sussex RH15 8NY
Tel: 01444 235694

Real Ales, Bar Food, Restaurant Menu,
Disabled Facilities

42 The Cross In Hand Inn

Cross In Hand, Heathfield, Sussex TN21 0SN
Tel: 01435 862053

Real Ales, Bar Food, Restaurant Menu,
No Smoking Area

43 Crow & Gate

Uckfield Road, Crowborough, Sussex TN6 3TA
Tel: 01892 603461

Real Ales, Bar Food, Restaurant Menu,
Accommodation, No Smoking Area, Disabled Facilities

44 The Crowborough Cross

Beacon Road, Crowborough, Sussex TN6 1AS
Tel: 01892 654009

Real Ales, Bar Food

45 The Crown

Carfax, Horsham, Sussex RH12 1DW
Tel: 01403 266350

Real Ales, Bar Food, Disabled Facilities

46 The Crown Inn
Church Road, Newick, Lewes, Sussex BN8 4JX
Tel: 01825 723293
Real Ales, Bar Food

47 The Crown Inn
Ifield Road, Crawley, Sussex RH11 7AS
Tel: 01293 520636
Bar Food, No Smoking Area

48 The Dog & Bacon
North Parade, Horsham, Sussex RH12 2QR
Tel: 01403 252176
Real Ales, Bar Food, No Smoking Area,
Disabled Facilities
See panel below

49 The Dog & Duck
Dorking Road, Horsham, Sussex RH12 3SA
Tel: 01306 627295
Real Ales, Bar Food, Restaurant Menu,
No Smoking Area

50 The Dolphin Pub
Wychpery Bower Butlers Green Road,
Haywards Heath, Sussex RH16 4AH
Tel: 01444 255921
Real Ales, Bar Food, Restaurant Menu,
No Smoking Area, Disabled Facilities

51 The Dorset Arms
Withyham, Nr Hartfield, Sussex TN7 4BD
Tel: 01892 770278
Real Ales, Bar Food, Restaurant Menu,
No Smoking Area, Disabled Facilities
See panel on page 38

52 The Dorset Arms
High Street, East Grinstead, Sussex RH19 3DE
Tel: 01342 316363
Real Ales, Bar Food, Restaurant Menu,
No Smoking Area, Disabled Facilities

53 The Dorsten
Dorsten Square, Crawley, West Sussex RH11 8XW
Tel: 01293 542709
Disabled Facilities

48 The Dog & Bacon
North Parade, Horsham, West Sussex RH12 2QR
☎ 01403 252176

Real Ales, Bar Food, No Smoking Area,
Disabled Facilities

- By the junction of North Parade and Trafalgar Road on the western side of Horsham
- Sussex, Badger
- Light snacks and Sunday roast 12-3
- Golf Society
- Beer garden, car park
- Major cards accepted
- 12-11 (Sun 12-10.30)
- All the attractions of Horsham nearby

The Dog & Bacon is a cosy, friendly pub close to the A24 on the western side of Horsham. Andy and Emma Waller have worked hard since taking over the pub in November 2003, and their efforts have earned the praise of local residents as well as motorists and others stopping or passing through the town. Refurbished a year ago, the bars are light, airy and contemporary, and there's plenty of outside for warm days. Several real ales are always available, along with other beers, lagers, wines, spirits and soft drinks, and the food offering covers light bites, sandwiches and popular fish, meat and vegetarian dishes. The Dog & Bacon has a thriving social side, with quiz nights, darts and pétanque. It also has its own Golf Society.

51 The Dorset Arms

Withyham, nr Hartfield, East Sussex TN7 4BD
☎ 01892 770278 ⊙ www.dorset-arms.co.uk

Real Ales, Bar Food, Restaurant Menu, No Smoking
Area, Disabled Facilities

☛ On the B2110 2 miles east of Hartfield

🍺 Harveys

🍴 12-3 (not Mon) & 7.30-11 (not Sun, Mon)

♫ Quiz 1st Wed of month

🪑 Garden, car park

💳 Major cards except Amex

🕐 11.30-3 (not Mon; Sun from 12) & 7.30-11
(not Sun, Mon)

🏛 Forest Way Walk and Cycle Route,
Groombridge Place 2 miles, Ashdown Forest
4 miles

One of the flagships of Harveys of Lewes, the Dorset Arms has that brewery's youngest licensee in Peter Randall. In a picturesque setting close to the Forest Way Country Walk and Cycle route, the inn was built as a farmhouse in the mid-16th century, and the interior is rich in historic appeal. This is a family affair par excellence: Peter's father and brother run the bar, where the full range of Harveys ales is available, and Peter's mother is the cook. Locally sourced ingredients are the basis of a wide range of dishes, from classics such as cottage pie, salmon fishcakes and rumpsteak to 1-, 2- or 3-course dinners with typical main courses including breast of chicken in a tangy lemon sauce, seared scallops with bacon and onions and the inn's celebrated half-shoulder of English lamb.

54 The Dragon

Colgate, nr Horsham, West Sussex RH12 4SY
☎ 01293 851206

Real Ales, Bar Food, Restaurant Menu

☛ Off the A264 east of Horsham and southwest
of Crawley

🍺 Sussex, Badger First Gold, Tanglefoot

🍴 12-2 & 6-9 (Sun 12-6)

🪑 Car park, garden

💳 Major cards except Amex

🕐 Lunchtime and evening (all day Fri, Sat & Sun)

🏛 Buchan Country Park 1 mile, Crawley 3 miles,
Horsham 3 miles

In November 2005 Tristan Toulmin took over the tenancy of the Dragon, a welcoming country pub off the A264 between Crawley and Horsham. Behind the handsome frontage – whitewashed below, redbrick and red-tiled above – the bar is a delightful spot to relax over a glass of one of the 4 real ales which are always available.

Food is an important part of the Dragon's business, and professional chefs prepare a fine selection of dishes both traditional and more adventurous, available from the printed menu or the specials board. Booking is advisable at all times.

There is a large well-kept beer garden, and occasional live entertainment and quiz nights. Children welcome.

54 The Dragon

Forest Road, Colgate, Sussex RH12 4SY
Tel: 01293 851206

Real Ales, Bar Food, Restaurant Menu

See panel opposite

55 Dun Horse Inn

Brighton Road, Mannings Heath, Horsham,
Sussex RH13 6HZ
Tel: 01403 265783

Real Ales, Bar Food, Restaurant Menu,
Accommodation, No Smoking Area

56 The Eight Bells

The Street, Bolney, Haywards Heath,
Sussex RH17 5QW
Tel: 01444 881396

Real Ales, Bar Food, Restaurant Menu,
No Smoking Area, Disabled Facilities

See panel below

57 Farmers Inn

Lewes Road, Scayne'S Hill, Haywards Heath,
Sussex RH17 7NE
Tel: 01444 831419

Real Ales, Bar Food, Restaurant Menu,
No Smoking Area, Disabled Facilities

58 The Firemans Arms

Five Ash Down, Nr Uckfield, Sussex TN22 3AN
Tel: 01825 732191

Real Ales, Bar Food, Restaurant Menu,
No Smoking Area, Disabled Facilities

See panel on page 40

59 Five Ashes Inn

Five Ashes, Mayfield, Sussex TN20 6HY
Tel: 01825 830485

Real Ales, Bar Food, Restaurant Menu,
No Smoking Area

---

56 The Eight Bells

The Street, Bolney, nr Haywards Heath,
West Sussex RH17 5QW

☎ 01444 881396

Real Ales, Bar Food, Restaurant Menu, No Smoking
Area, Disabled Facilities

- Off the A272 near junction with A23
- Harveys and other local brews
- 12-2.30 & 6-9.30
- Car park
- Major cards accepted
- 11-11
- Hickstead 2 miles, Haywards Heath 6 miles

Business partners David Cunningham and Phil Dooley left a very busy pub in Brighton to take over the **Eight Bells** in May 2005. David, front of house, and Phil at the stoves have put their talents to excellent use in their new venture, a traditional village pub dating back as far as 1581. Eight 'real' bells –

not just a painting – make a very distinctive pub sign, and the smartly refurbished interior is a splendidly inviting spot for enjoying a drink or a meal in relaxed, civilised surroundings. Phil's menu makes mouthwatering reading – smoked boned quail with balsamic pickled eggs, smoked haddock in herb-scented pancakes, sea bass stuffed with lemon and herb butter, veal & ham pie – and results on the plate really do live up to the tempting descriptions. And room should definitely be left for one (at least!) of Phil's super desserts.

58 The Firemans Arms Freehouse & Restaurant

Five Ash Down, nr Uckfield, East Sussex TN22 3AN
☎ 01825 732191

Real Ales, Bar Food, Restaurant Menu,
No Smoking Area, Disabled Facilities

☛ I mile N of Uckfield by the junction of the A26 and A272

🍺 Harveys plus Guest Ale

🍴 12-2 & 6.30-9 (not Tues eve) Sunday Roasts, non smoking restaurant.

🎵 Quiz first Tues of month, 'open mike' last Tues of month

⚓ Beer garden, car park

💳 Major cards accepted

🕐 11.30-3 & 5-11 (all day Sat & Sun)

🏛 Uckfield 1 mile

The **Firemans Arms** is a very distinctive gabled redbrick building with considerable traditional appeal. Martin Cook, well established as the landlord of this deservedly popular pub, is also the chef, and his home-cooked dishes have won a strong local following. All the time-honoured pub classics are on the menu, but also plenty of less familiar choices typified by crab and cayenne cakes, smoked haddock in Guinness batter, gnocchi in a spinach and pesto cream sauce, lamb & leek casserole, rabbit & bacon pie and fresh fish at the weekend. Sandwiches and light snacks are available. Harveys Sussex Best is the resident cask ale, and the pub also keeps some excellent cask ciders. The Firemans Arms hosts a quiz on the first Tuesday of the month, while on the last Tuesday inhibitions are cast aside on 'open mike' night.

60 Foresters Arms

Fairwarp, Ashdown Forest, Uckfield,
Sussex TN22 3BP
Tel: 01825 712808

Real Ales, Bar Food, Restaurant Menu,
No Smoking Area, Disabled Facilities

61 Foresters Arms

43 St Leonards Road, Horsham,
Sussex RH13 6EH
Tel: 01403 254458

Real Ales, No Smoking Area

62 The Foresters Arms

19 Hartfield Road, Forest Row,
Sussex RH18 5DN
Tel: 01342 826398

Real Ales, Bar Food, Restaurant Menu,
No Smoking Area, Disabled Facilities

63 Fountain Inn

High Street, Handcross, Haywards Heath,
Sussex RH17 6BJ
Tel: 01444 400218

Real Ales, Bar Food, Restaurant Menu,
No Smoking Area

64 The Fountain Inn

81 Rusper Road, Roffey, Horsham,
Sussex RH12 4BJ
Tel: 01403 255428

Real Ales, Bar Food, Restaurant Menu,
No Smoking Area

See panel opposite

65 Fox & Hounds

Fox Hill, Haywards Heath, Sussex RH16 4QY
Tel: 01444 413342

Real Ales, Bar Food, Restaurant Menu,
No Smoking Area, Disabled Facilities

64 The Fountain Inn

81 Rusper Road, Roffey,,Horsham,
West Sussex RH12 4BJ
☎ 01405 255248

Real Ales, Bar Food, Restaurant Menu,
No Smoking Area

- On the Rusper Road out of Horsham
- Sussex, Badger
- Bar and Restaurant L & D
- Sunday quiz
- Garden, car park
- Major cards accepted
- 11-11 (Sun 12-10.30)
- Horsham's attractions close by; Rusper 3 miles, Gatwick Airport 7 miles

The **Fountain** is a fine roadside inn on the Rusper Road out of Horsham. The interior of the inn is strikingly contemporary, with lightwood furniture on tiled floors, while outside there's plenty of seating in the large garden. The Fountain is a great place for a snack or a meal, with a choice of bar and restaurant menus served lunchtime and evening. The main menu, 'Francesco @ the Fountain, features Italian and European specialities, typified by spaghetti (Bolognese sauce, meatballs, or lemon chilli prawns), pepper steak, paella for 2 and chicken & pepper skewers with rosemary. Baked-to-order pizzas are very popular, with a choice of almost 20 toppings to mix and match. The Fountain is also one of the town's most sociable spots, with pool, darts, bar billiards, monthly karaoke, Sky Sports TV and a golf society.

66 The Gardeners Arms

Seisfield Road, Ardingly, Haywards Heath,
Sussex RH17 6TJ
Tel: 01444 892328

Real Ales, Bar Food, Restaurant Menu,
No Smoking Area

67 The Gate

Rusper Road , Ifield, Crawley, Sussex RH11 0LQ
Tel: 01293 871271

Real Ales, Bar Food, Restaurant Menu,
No Smoking Area, Disabled Facilities

See panel on page 42

68 Gatwick Manor

London Road, Lowfield Heath, Crawley,
Sussex RH10 9ST
Tel: 01293 526301

Real Ales, Bar Food, Restaurant Menu,
Accommodation, No Smoking Area, Disabled Facilities

69 The George & Dragon

Dragons Lane, Shipley, Horsham, Sussex RH13 9JE
Tel: 01403 741320

Real Ales, Bar Food, Restaurant Menu,
No Smoking Area, Disabled Facilities

70 The George Hotel

High Street, Crawley, Sussex RH10 1BS
Tel: 01293 524215

Real Ales, Bar Food, Accommodation,
No Smoking Area, Disabled Facilities

71 Ghyll Manor

High Street, Rusper, Sussex RH124PX
Tel: 01293 871571

Bar Food, Restaurant Menu, Accommodation,
No Smoking Area, Disabled Facilities

67 **The Gate**

Ifield, nr Crawley, West Sussex RH11 0LQ
☎ 01293 871271 Fax: 01293 871271

Real Ales, Bar Food, Restaurant Menu,
No Smoking Area, Disabled Facilities

- Off the Rusper road 1½ miles from Crawley
- Hall & Woodhouse
- 12-2.30 & 7-9.30, 12-9 Sun, large specials board, full menu & snacks menu.
- Quiz every other Wednesday
- Garden, car park
- Major cards accepted
- 11.30-3 & 6-11, 12-10.30 Sunday
- Crawley 1½ miles, Gatwick 4 miles

The Gate, which enjoys a pleasant rural setting off the Rusper road out of Crawley, is an early 18th century inn of great character. One end of the redbrick building is covered with creeper, and masses of flowers make a colourful show in spring and summer. The bar and dining areas are comfortable and traditional, and the pub has a lovely beer garden at the side and back, with barbecues and bonfire nights a regular feature. The food here is some of the best in the region, and tenants Lorna and Graham and their chef are kept busy satisfying customers who come to enjoy anything from a light snack (served all day) to a three-course meal. The choice really is impressive, from dressed crab, burgers, cauliflower cheese and cup mushrooms filled with ratatouille to super pies (steak & stilton, lamb & mint), smoked haddock florentine, half-shoulder of lamb and a mighty mixed grill.

72 The Golden Eagle

America Lane, Haywards Heath, Sussex RH16 3QB
Tel: 01444 456826

Real Ales

73 The Grange Hotel

15 Brighton Road, Crawley, Sussex RH10 6AE
Tel: 01293 403467

Real Ales, Bar Food, Restaurant Menu,
Accommodation, No Smoking Area

74 The Grapes

Old Brighton Road South, Pease Pottage, Crawley,
Sussex RH11 9AH
Tel: 01293 526359

Real Ales, Bar Food, Restaurant Menu,
Disabled Facilities

75 Green Man

The Green, Horsted Keynes, Sussex RH17 7AS
Tel: 01825 790656

Real Ales, Bar Food, No Smoking Area

76 The Green Man

Jolesfield, Partridge Green, Horsham,
Sussex RH13 8JT
Tel: 01403 710250

Real Ales, Bar Food, Restaurant Menu

77 The Greets Inn

47 Friday Street, Horsham, Sussex RH12 3QY
Tel: 01403 265047

Real Ales, Restaurant Menu, No Smoking Area

78 The Greyhound

Radford Road, Tinsley Green, Crawley,
Sussex RH10 3NS
Tel: 01293 884220

Real Ales, Bar Food, Restaurant Menu

79 Griffin Inn

Fletching, Uckfield, East Sussex TN22 3SS
Tel: 01825 722890

Real Ales, Bar Food, Restaurant Menu,
Accommodation, No Smoking Area, Disabled Facilities

82 The Half Moon

Haywards Heath Road, Balcombe,
West Sussex RH17 6PA
☎ 01444 811582

Real Ales, Bar Food, Restaurant Menu,
No Smoking Area

☛ Midway between Crawley and Haywards
Heath on the B2036

🍺 Harveys Wessex Best

🍴 12-2.30 & 6-9.30 (no food Mon eve)

🏍 Major cards except Amex and Diners

🕐 Lunchtime and evening (all day Saturday)

🏛 Balcombe Viaduct nearby; Crawley 4 miles,
Haywards Heath 4 miles

The area around the **Half Moon** is
excellent walking country, and this fine old
inn is the perfect choice to cater for fresh-air
thirsts and appetites. Built in 1735 the
unbroken tradition of hospitality dates back
some 270 years. Behind the attractive
whitewashed frontage, with yellow door and
window surrounds and colourful hanging
baskets, the bar and restaurant have well-
maintained period appeal, creating a delightful
ambience for enjoying a drink or a meal. The
printed menu and specials board tempt with a
good across-the-board choice that includes
game dishes in their season. Booking is
recommended at the weekend. The Half Moon
is very much at the social heart of the village
of Balcombe, which lies on the B2036
between Crawley and Haywards Heath. An
eyecatching local feature is Balcombe Viaduct,
which carries the London-Brighton railway line
across the Ouse Valley.

80 The Half Moon

Friars Gate, Crowborough, Sussex TN6 1XB
Tel: 01892 661270

Real Ales, Bar Food, Restaurant Menu,
Disabled Facilities

81 The Half Moon

The Street, Haywards Heath, Sussex RH17 5TR
Tel: 01444 461227

Real Ales, Bar Food, Restaurant Menu,
No Smoking Area

82 The Half Moon

Haywards Heath Road, Balcombe,
Sussex RH17 6PA
Tel: 01444 811582

Real Ales, Bar Food, Restaurant Menu,
No Smoking Area

See panel above

83 The Hare & Hounds

The Street, Framfield, Uckfield, Sussex TN22 5NJ
Tel: 01825 890327

Real Ales, Bar Food, Disabled Facilities

84 The Hatch Inn

Colmans Hatch, Hartfield, Sussex TN7 4EJ
Tel: 01342 822363

Real Ales, Bar Food, Restaurant Menu,
No Smoking Area, Disabled Facilities

85 Haywaggon Inn

High Street, Hartfield, Sussex TN7 4AB
Tel: 01892 770252

Real Ales, Restaurant Menu, No Smoking Area,
Disabled Facilities

86 The Heath

47 Sussex Road, Haywards Heath,
Sussex RH16 4DZ
Tel: 01444 413766

Real Ales, Bar Food, Restaurant Menu

87 The Hedgehog Inn

Effingham Rd, Copthorne, Crawley,
West Sussex   RH10 3HY
Tel: 08703 305175

Bar Food, Restaurant Menu, Accommodation,
No Smoking Area, Disabled Facilities

88 Hickstead Hotel

Jobs Lane, Bolney, Nr Burgess Hill, Sussex   RH17 5NZ
Tel: 01444 248023

Bar Food, Restaurant Menu, Accommodation,
No Smoking Area, Disabled Facilities

89 The Highlands Inn

Lewes Road, Uckfield, Sussex   TN22 5TB
Tel: 01825 762989

Real Ales, Bar Food, Restaurant Menu,
No Smoking Area, Disabled Facilities

90 The Hillside Inn

Balcombe Road, Pound Hill, Crawley,
Sussex   RH10 7SX
Tel: 01293 880910

Real Ales, Bar Food, Restaurant Menu,
No Smoking Area, Disabled Facilities

91 The Holmbush Inn

Faygate Lane, Fayegate, Horsham, Sussex   RH12 4SH
Tel: 01293 851539

Real Ales, Bar Food, Restaurant Menu,
No Smoking Area, Disabled Facilities

92 The Hornbrook Inn

Brighton Road, Horsham, Sussex   RH13 6QA
Tel: 01403 252638

Real Ales, Bar Food, Restaurant Menu,
No Smoking Area, Disabled Facilities

93 Horse 'N' Groom

East Street, Horsham, Sussex   RH12 1HH
Tel: 01403 253924

94 The Intrepid Fox

West Holey, East Grinstead, Sussex   RH19 4EE
Tel: 01342 810644

Real Ales, Bar Food, Restaurant Menu,
No Smoking Area

95 J.D Wetherspoon

King St, East Grinstead, West Sussex   RH19 3DJ
Tel: 01342 335130

Real Ales, Bar Food, Restaurant Menu,
No Smoking Area, Disabled Facilities

96 Ja Ja Bar

26 High St, Crawley, West Sussex   RH10 1BH
Tel: 01293 520220

Bar Food, Restaurant Menu, No Smoking Area,
Disabled Facilities

97 Jolly Tanners

Handcross Road, Staplefield, Sussex   RH17 6EE
Tel: 01444 400335

Real Ales, Bar Food, Restaurant Menu,
No Smoking Area, Disabled Facilities

98 The Jubilee Oak

6 High Street, Crawley, Sussex   RH10 1BU
Tel: 01293 565335

Real Ales, Bar Food, Restaurant Menu,
No Smoking Area, Disabled Facilities

99 Kings Arms

24 High Street, Crowborough, Sussex   TN6 3LJ
Tel: 01892 853441

Real Ales, Bar Food, Restaurant Menu,
Accommodation, No Smoking Area, Disabled Facilities

100 The Kings Arms

64 Bishop Road, Horsham, Sussex   RH12 1QN
Tel: 01403 253588

Real Ales, Bar Food, Accommodation,
Disabled Facilities

101 The Kings Head

East Grinstead Road, North Chailey, Lewes,
Sussex   BN8 4DH
Tel: 01825 722870

Real Ales, Bar Food, Restaurant Menu,
No Smoking Area, Disabled Facilities

102 The Lamb Inn

Lambs Green Lane, Rusper, Horsham,
Sussex   RH12 4RG
Tel: 01293 871336

Real Ales, Bar Food, Restaurant Menu,
No Smoking Area, Disabled Facilities

103 Linden Tree

47 High Street, Lindfield, Sussex RH16 2HN
Tel: 01444 482995

Real Ales

104 Lynd Cross

Springfield Road, Horsham, Sussex RH12 2PG
Tel: 01403 272393

Real Ales, Bar Food, Restaurant Menu,
No Smoking Area, Disabled Facilities

105 Maid Of Sussex

Gales Drive, Crawley, Sussex RH10 1QA
Tel: 01293 525404

Real Ales, Bar Food, Disabled Facilities

106 Malt Shovel

15 Springfield Road, Horsham, Sussex RH12 2PG
Tel: 01403 254543

Real Ales, Bar Food

107 Maypole Inn

Hurstwood Road, High Hurstwood, Uckfield,
Sussex TN22 4AH
Tel: 01825 732257

Real Ales, Bar Food, Restaurant Menu,
No Smoking Area, Disabled Facilities

108 The Mill House

Hyde Drive, Crawley, Sussex RH11 0PL
Tel: 01293 534959

Restaurant Menu, No Smoking Area,
Disabled Facilities

109 Moon Maker

199 Three Bridges Road, Crawley, Sussex RH10 1LG
Tel: 01293 540338

Real Ales

110 The Nelson

25 Trafalgar Road, Horsham, Sussex RH12 2QD
Tel: 01403 242783

Real Ales

111 Norfolk Arms

Crawley Road, Horsham, Sussex RH12 4NB
Tel: 01403 264913

Real Ales, Bar Food, No Smoking Area,
Disabled Facilities

112 The Nutley Arms

London Rd, Fords Green Nutley, Uckfield,
East Sussex TN22 3LJ
Tel: 01825 713322

Real Ales, Bar Food, Restaurant Menu,
Accommodation, No Smoking Area, Disabled Facilities

See panel on page 46

113 The Oak Barn Restaurant & Bar

Cuckfield Road, Burgess Hill, Sussex RH15 8RE
Tel: 01444 258222

Real Ales, Bar Food, Restaurant Menu,
No Smoking Area, Disabled Facilities

See panel on page 46

114 Oak Inn

Street Lane, Haywards Heath, Sussex RH17 6UA
Tel: 01444 892244

Real Ales, Bar Food, Restaurant Menu,
No Smoking Area

115 The Old Punch Bowl

101 High Street, Crawley, Sussex RH10 1DD
Tel: 01293 529085

Real Ales, Bar Food, Restaurant Menu,
Accommodation, No Smoking Area, Disabled Facilities

116 Orange Square

52-54 The Broadway, Haywards Heath,
West Sussex RH16 3AL
Tel: 01444 456666

Real Ales

117 The Parsons Pig

Balcombe Road, Crawley, Sussex RH10 3NL
Tel: 01293 883104

Real Ales, Bar Food, Restaurant Menu,
No Smoking Area, Disabled Facilities

112 The Nutley Arms

London Road (A22), Fords Green, Nutley,
nr Uckfield, East Sussex TN22 3LJ

☎ 01825 713322 Fax: 01825 713999

🌐 www.nutleyarmspub.co.uk

e-mail: nutleyarms.pub@btopenworld.com

Real Ales, Bar Food, Restaurant Menu, Accommodation, No Smoking Area, Disabled Facilities

☞ On the A22 8 miles below East Grinstead or Uckfield

🍴 12-3 & 6-9.30 (no food Sun eve)

🎵 Quiz last Tuesday of the month

🚗 Car park

💳 Major cards accepted

🕐 10am-11pm

🏛 Ashdown Forest 2 miles, Crowborough 4 miles, Bluebell Railway 4 miles

The Greek landlord and French landlady add a delightfully cosmopolitan feel to the Nutley Arms, their popular pub and restaurant on the A22 London Road just below Ashdown Forest. A substantial redbrick building, it has a well-furnished interior with plenty of space to relax over a drink or a meal, and when the sun shines the large garden comes into its own. The pub is open all day for drinks, and food is served every session except Sunday evening. The menu offers a good choice of mainly familiar classics such as steaks, scampi, spaghetti and fish cakes, but a particular speciality of the house is a variety of tasty, juicy kebabs – doner, shish, kofta and chicken – available in two sizes to eat in or take away. The Nutley Arms is a popular venue for parties and get-togethers, as well as being a great favourite with families.

113 The Oak Barn Restaurant & Bar

Cuckfield Road, Burgess Hill, West Sussex RH15 8RE

☎ 01444 258222 🌐 www.oakbarnrestaurant.co.uk

Real Ales, Bar Food, Restaurant Menu, No Smoking Area, Disabled Facilities

☞ The inn lies off the B2036 between Burgess Hill and Ansty

🍺 Harveys, Ruddles

🍴 12-2.30 & 6.30-9 (snacks all day)

🎵 Golf club

🚗 Garden, patio, car park

💳 Major cards accepted

🕐 10am – 11pm

🏛 Haywards Heath 3 miles, Hickstead 3 miles

Owner Chris Collins has invested a great deal of time and money in creating the Oak Barn Restaurant & Bar in a wonderfully atmospheric setting between Burgess Hill and Ansty. The classic oak barn that houses the restaurant retains original beams and rafters, and a huge wagon wheel is suspended from the ceiling; outside, picnic benches under parasols provide a delightful alfresco alternative when the sun shines. The main menu has something for everyone, from sandwiches, baguettes and jacket potatoes to a wide variety of fish, meat and vegetarian main courses, grills and Oak Barn favourites such as Thai fish cakes, steak & ale pie, lasagne, chilli con carne and home-cooked ham, egg & fries. A well-annotated wine list includes several wines available by the glass. The Oak Barn is also a lovely spot for morning coffee and afternoon tea, and a private room is available for meetings and functions. The site includes a golf club and driving range.

118 Peacock Inn

Shortbridge, Piltdown, Uckfield, Sussex TN22 3XA
Tel: 01825 762463

Real Ales, Bar Food, Restaurant Menu,
No Smoking Area

119 Pelham Buckle

216 Ifield Drive, Crawley, West Sussex RH11 0DR
Tel: 01293 525412

120 The Piltdown Man

Piltdown, Uckfield, Sussex TN22 3XL
Tel: 01825 723563

Real Ales, Bar Food, Restaurant Menu,
Accommodation, No Smoking Area, Disabled Facilities

See panel below

121 Plough And Horses

Walshes Road, Crowborough, Sussex TN6 3RE
Tel: 01892 652614

Real Ales, Bar Food, Restaurant Menu,
Accommodation, No Smoking Area, Disabled Facilities

122 Plough Inn

Ifield Street, Ifield, Crawley, Sussex RH11 0NN
Tel: 01293 524292

Real Ales, Bar Food, Disabled Facilities

123 Plough Inn

High Street, Rusper, Horsham, Sussex RH12 4PX
Tel: 01293 871215

Real Ales, Bar Food, Restaurant Menu,
No Smoking Area

124 The Prince Albert

Copthorne Bank, Copthorne, Crawley,
Sussex RH10 3QU
Tel: 01342 712702

Real Ales, Bar Food

125 The Prince Of Wales

Lingfield Road, East Grinstead, Sussex RH19 2EQ
Tel: 01342 325703

Real Ales

---

120 The Piltdown Man

Lewes Road (A272), Piltdown, Uckfield,
East Sussex TN22 3XL
☎ 01825 723563

Real Ales, Bar Food, Restaurant Menu, Accommodation, No Smoking Area, Disabled Facilities

- ☛ On the A272 6 miles E of Haywards Heath
- ☕ Sussex Best, St Austell Tribute
- 🍴 Food served throughout opening times
- ⊨ 2 en suite rooms
- ♫ Live music Friday
- ⛺ Garden, children's play area, car park
- 💳 Major cards accepted
- ⏱ 12-3 & 6-11 (all day Fri, Sat & Sun)
- 🏛 Sheffield Park NT 2 miles, Uckfield 2 miles, Haywards Heath 6 miles

Piltdown Man, a cheerful roadside pub on the A272 east of Haywards Heath. The welcoming exterior is adorned with flowers and shrubs, while inside is equally appealing, with an open fire in a massive brick hearth, flagstone floors and sturdy old furniture. A selection of cask ales is always on tap, and for hungry visitors the choice, available whenever the pub is open, runs from light bites to home-cooked classics such as steak, pies, fish & chips and curries. The Piltdown Man has two en suite bedrooms for guests staying overnight.

The village of Piltdown hit the headlines in 1912 with the discovery of a 'missing link' between apes and humans. Many years later the find was exposed as a fake. The skull of that 'humanoid' is depicted on the sign of the

129 The Red Lion

Lewes Road, Chelwood Gate, Haywards Heath,
East Sussex RH17 7DE

☎ 01825 740265

Real Ales, Bar Food, Restaurant Menu,
No Smoking Area, Disabled Facilities

☛ On the A275 6 miles S of East Grinstead via
A27

🍺 Shepherd Neame Spitfire

🍴 Lunch & Dinner

🪑 Beer garden, car park

💳 Major cards accepted

🕐 11-11

🏛 Ashdown Forest 2 miles, Bluebell Railway 3
miles, Crowborough 6 miles

There are few better places for a meal in the whole region than the **Red Lion**, which stands by the A275 just below the junction with the A22. The history of the

building goes back as far as 1671, and it has never been in better form than in the care of the present tenants Ian and Karen Perry. They have a warm and genuine welcome for the whole family (and their dogs!) and have won back all the local trade as well as the many visitors and motorists who pass this way.

The bar, with its polished wooden floor and sturdy wooden furniture, has a lovely traditional feel, and the pub has lawned areas both at the front, with flowers and picnic benches, and at the back, with lots of attractive greenery and plenty more tables and chairs. With a seasonally changing menu as exciting as

the Red Lion's, the reputation of an eating place depends on the team in the kitchen, and here they succeed triumphantly with every dish, whether it's a light snack, a family favourite or one of the kitchen's many imaginative and original creations.

The menus really do offer something for everyone. Snacks include filled baguettes, jacket potatoes and ploughman's platters and light bites like deep-fried wedges with cheese & bacon, creamy mushrooms with garlic bread and a salad of sun-blush tomato, roasted red onion and peppers. 'Family Favourites' include gammon & pineapple, crab omelette, cottage pie and chicken tikka masala, and there are some very interesting pasta dishes. The kitchen spreads its wings with superb main courses such as roasted cod on ratatouille provençale, or slow-roasted belly of pork in soy and orange, with lemon and sage potatoes and a fennel, orange and pineapple salsa. Scrumptious desserts – all home-made – keep the enjoyment level sky-high to the end.

Definitely a place to seek out among the many places of interest in the vicinity, which include Ashdown Forest, the Nutley Windmill, the National Trust's Sheffield Park Garden and the Bluebell Railway.

126 The Queens Head

Chapel Road, Barns Green, nr Horsham,
West Sussex RH13 0PS
☎ 01403 730436

Real Ales, Bar Food, Restaurant Menu,
No Smoking Area, Disabled Facilities

 3 miles S of Horsham off the A24 or A264

 Sussex, Horsham, London Pride

12-2 & 7-9 (not Sun eve)

Quiz Sunday evening

Off-road parking, beer garden

Major cards except Diners

Lunchtime and Evening, all day Sunday

Billingshurst 2 miles, Horsham 3 miles

In a village a short drive south of Horsham, the **Queens Head** is a marvellous country inn developed from two 18th century cottages that were once the homes of smugglers. Colourful flowers adorn the façade, and the inn has a pleasant patio at the front and a lawned garden at the back. Inside, it's quaint and inviting, with low ceilings, heavy black beams and a variety of pew benches, settees and comfortably upholstered seats. An inglenook fire adds an extra cosy feel in the cooler months. Mine hosts John and Lucy Pullinger are enhancing the inn's reputation for hospitality and good cheer with a trio of real ales and a regularly changing menu that offers something for everyone, including fish & chips on Wednesday evening and superb fresh fish specials at the weekend. Booking is advisable for Friday and Saturday evenings, the Sunday carvery and the regular themed food evenings. Families are welcome, and there's a play area for little ones in the garden.

126 The Queens Head

Chapel Road, Barns Green, Horsham,
Sussex RH13 0PS
Tel: 01403 730436

Real Ales, Bar Food, Restaurant Menu,
No Smoking Area, Disabled Facilities

See panel above

127 The Queens Head

37 Queen Street, Horsham, Sussex RH13 5AA
Tel: 01403 252721

Real Ales, Bar Food, Restaurant Menu,
Accommodation, No Smoking Area, Disabled Facilities

128 Rat & Parrot

91 High St, Crawley, West Sussex RH10 1BA
Tel: 01293 550928

Bar Food, No Smoking Area, Disabled Facilities

129 The Red Lion

Lewes Road, Chelwood Gate, Haywards Heath,
Sussex RH17 7DE
Tel: 01825 740265

Real Ales, Bar Food, Restaurant Menu,
No Smoking Area, Disabled Facilities

See panel opposite

130 The Red Lion

Lion Lane, Turners Hill, Sussex RH10 4NU
Tel: 01342 715416

Real Ales, Bar Food, Disabled Facilities

See panel on page 50

131 The Red Lion

High St, Lindfield, Haywards Heath, West Sussex RH16 2HL
Tel: 01444 487000

Real Ales, Bar Food, Restaurant Menu,
No Smoking Area

130 The Red Lion

Lion Lane, Turner's Hill, nr East Grinstead,
West Sussex RH10 4NU

☎ 01342 715416

Real Ales, Bar Food, Disabled Facilities

☞ Off the B2110, off the A264 4 miles W of East Grinstead

🍺 Harveys

🍴 L only 12-2.15 (not Sun)

♫ Quiz every other Thurs in winter

⚒ Car park

💳 Major cards accepted

🕐 11-3 & 5.30-11 (Sun 12-10.30)

🏛 Wakehurst Place NT 3 miles, Crawley 5 miles, East Grinstead 5 miles

Hosts Ashley and Elaine are proud to describe the Red Lion as a 'proper pub' serving real ales from Harveys, a good range of wines and spirits, and straightforward dishes available at Lunchtime Monday to Saturday. The Grade II listed building is a classic village pub with a warm, convivial atmosphere and invitingly old-fashioned décor. In the winter months log fires keep things cosy on the bar, while in summer picnic tables are set out among the flowers and shrubs at the front of the pub, and in the large beer garden at the back. The food choice takes in croques madame and monsieur, jacket potatoes, fish cakes, ham & eggs and chilli con carne. The pleasant, unpretentious ambience makes the Red Lion a popular venue for parties and functions.

132 The Red Lyon

The Street, Slinfold, West Sussex RH13 0RR

☎ 01403 790339 🌐 www.theredlyon.co.uk

Real Ales, Bar Food, Restaurant Menu, Accommodation, No Smoking Area

☞ Off the A29 5 miles N of Billingshurst, or off A264 2 miles W of Horsham

🍺 Harveys, Greene King IPA, Adnams, London Pride

🍴 Lunch & Dinner, light snacks all day

🛏 4 rooms (3 en suite)

⚒ Garden, car park

💳 Major cards accepted

🕐 12-3 & 6-11 (all day Fri, Sat & Sun)

🏛 Horsham 2 miles, Billingshurst 5 miles

Lying just a short drive from both the A24 and the A264, the Red Lyon is an ideal stop for business people and leisure visitors as well as being a local favourite. First mentioned as an ale house in 1687, its history begins several centuries earlier, and in its time the building has been known as Nibletts and the Kings Head before the current hosts Kevin and Simon re-adopted its original name. They have firmly re-established its reputation as a splendid village pub with great food, excellent ales and four well-appointed en suite rooms for B&B guests. In the handsomely decorated oak-panelled restaurant customers can enjoy anything from a sandwich or a salad to steakburgers, chunky chilli, fillet of lamb in puff pastry, layered pancakes and roasted vegetable bake, and seafood brochettes with a Thai curry sauce. At the back of the pub is a lovely garden where parents can enjoy the fresh air and watch their children playing in safety.

132 **The Red Lyon**

The Street, Slinfold, Horsham, Sussex RH13 0RR
Tel: 01403 790339

Real Ales, Bar Food, Restaurant Menu,
Accommodation, No Smoking Area

See panel opposite

133 **Regency**

Old Hollow Worth, Copthorne, Crawley,
Sussex RH10 4TA
Tel: 01293 887433

Real Ales, Bar Food, Restaurant Menu,
Accommodation, No Smoking Area

134 **The Rising Sun**

Pondtail Road, Horsham, Sussex RH12 2NJ
Tel: 01403 253463

Real Ales, Bar Food, No Smoking Area

135 **The Rose & Crown**

High Street, East Grinstead, Sussex RH19 3DD
Tel: 01342 322176

Real Ales, Bar Food, Restaurant Menu,
No Smoking Area

136 **The Rose & Crown**

Fletching, Uckfield, Sussex TN22 3ST
Tel: 01825 722039

Real Ales, Bar Food, Accommodation,
No Smoking Area, Disabled Facilities

137 **Royal Oak**

Ifield Green, Ifield, Crawley,
West Sussex RH11 0ND
Tel: 01293 544444

Real Ales, Bar Food, No Smoking Area

138 **Royal Oak**

Wineham Lane, Wineham, Henfield,
Sussex BN5 9AY
Tel: 01444 881252

Real Ales, Bar Food, No Smoking Area

139 **The Royal Oak**

Friday Street, Rusper, Horsham, Sussex RH12 4QA
Tel: 01293 871393

Real Ales, Bar Food

140 **The Royal Oak**

1 Church Road, Lewes, Sussex BN8 4JU
Tel: 01825 722506

Real Ales, Bar Food

141 **The Royal Oak**

Grange Road, Crawley, Sussex RH10 4JT
Tel: 01342 713170

Real Ales, Bar Food, Restaurant Menu,
No Smoking Area, Disabled Facilities

142 **The Royal Oak**

Jacobs Post, Ditchling Common, Burgess Hill,
Sussex RH15 0SJ
Tel: 01444 471263

Real Ales, Bar Food, Restaurant Menu,
No Smoking Area

143 **The Selsey Arms**

Coolham, Horsham, Sussex RH13 8QJ
Tel: 01403 741537

Real Ales, Bar Food, Restaurant Menu,
Accommodation, No Smoking Area

See panel on page 52

144 **Ship Inn**

Whitemans Green, Cuckfield, Haywards Heath,
Sussex RH17 5BY
Tel: 01444 413219

Real Ales, Bar Food, Restaurant Menu,
Accommodation, No Smoking Area, Disabled Facilities

145 **Ship Inn**

Ship Street, East Grinstead, Sussex RH19 4EG
Tel: 01342 312089

Real Ales, Bar Food, Restaurant Menu,
Accommodation, No Smoking Area, Disabled Facilities

146 **Singapore Sam Plc**

County Mall, Crawley, Sussex RH10 1FF
Tel: 01293 532273

Restaurant Menu, Disabled Facilities

147 **Sloop Inn**

Sloop Lane, Scayne'S Hill, Haywards Heath,
Sussex RH17 7NP
Tel: 01444 831219

Real Ales, Bar Food, Restaurant Menu,
No Smoking Area, Disabled Facilities

143 The Selsey Arms

Coolham, Horsham, West Sussex RH13 8QJ
☎ 01403 741537

Real Ales, Bar Food, Restaurant Menu,
Accommodation, No Smoking Area

- At the junction of the A272 and B2139 3 miles E of Billingshurst
- Harveys Sussex Best
- 12-3.15 & 6.30-9.30
- 4 rooms en suite
- Garden, car park
- Major cards accepted
- 11-11 (Sun 12-10.30)
- Billingshurst 3 miles, Shipley Mill 2 miles, Horsham 8 miles

Three miles east of Billingshurst, where the A272 meets the B2139, the **Selsey Arms** has all the qualities associated with a classic English country pub. Tradition is king here, from the old-world décor with low ceilings, stone or wooden floors and huge open fires to the well-kept ales and the classic home cooking – and some of the friendly, hard-working staff even sport splendid bow ties! Harveys Sussex Best, Flowers IPA and Fullers London Pride are on tap to quench thirsts, and the food, served every lunchtime and evening, caters for all appetites, ranging from sandwiches and baked potatoes at the bar to smoked haddock topped with a poached egg, Selsey crab and lobster, home-made steak & onion pie, beef and gammon steaks, liver & bacon and a hunger-busting mixed grill. The beer gardens provide a lovely spot for alfresco eating and drinking, and four excellent en suite bedrooms cater for overnight guests.

148 The Snooty Fox

Haslett Avenue West, Crawley, Sussex RH10 1LY
Tel: 01293 619759

Real Ales, Bar Food, No Smoking Area,
Disabled Facilities

149 The Snowdrop Inn

Snowdrop Lane, Haywards Heath, Sussex RH16 2QE
Tel: 01444 412259

Real Ales, Bar Food, Restaurant Menu,
No Smoking Area

150 The Sportsman Wine Bar

9-11 Cantelupe Road, East Grinstead,
Sussex RH19 3BE
Tel: 01342 311944

Real Ales, Bar Food, Accommodation

151 St Leonards Arms

49 Brighton Road, Horsham, Sussex RH13 6EZ
Tel: 01403 261661

Bar Food, Restaurant Menu, No Smoking Area

152 Star

1 The Broadway, Haywards Heath,
Sussex RH16 3AQ
Tel: 01444 413267

Real Ales, Bar Food

153 The Star

Crawley Road, Roffey, Horsham, Sussex RH12 4DT
Tel: 01403 259890

Real Ales

154 The Star Inn

Horsham Road, Horsham, Sussex RH12 4RA
Tel: 01293 871264

Real Ales, Bar Food, Restaurant Menu,
No Smoking Area, Disabled Facilities

155 The Star Inn

London Road, Felbridge, East Grinstead,
Sussex RH19 2QR
Tel: 01342 323239

Real Ales, Bar Food, Restaurant Menu,
No Smoking Area, Disabled Facilities

156 Sussex Barn
North Heath Lane, Little Haven, Horsham,
Sussex RH12 5PJ
Tel: 01403 270406
Real Ales, Bar Food, Restaurant Menu,
No Smoking Area, Disabled Facilities

157 Sussex Oak
2 Church Street, Warnham, Horsham,
Sussex RH12 3QW
Tel: 01403 265028
Real Ales, Bar Food, Restaurant Menu,
No Smoking Area, Disabled Facilities

158 Sussex Oak
Blackham, Sussex TN3 9UA
Tel: 01892 740273
Real Ales, Bar Food, Restaurant Menu,
No Smoking Area, Disabled Facilities

159 The Swan
Lewes Road, Forest Row, Sussex RH18 5ER
Tel: 01342 822318
Real Ales, Restaurant Menu, No Smoking Area,
Disabled Facilities

160 Swan Inn
Horsham Road, West Green, Crawley,
Sussex RH11 7LY
Tel: 01293 527447
Real Ales

161 Talbot Inn
High Street, Haywards Heath, Sussex RH17 5JX
Tel: 01444 413137
Real Ales

162 The Tanners Arms
78 Brighton Road, Horsham, Sussex RH13 5BU
Tel: 01403 250527
Real Ales, Bar Food

163 Tavern On The Green
Peter House Parade, Pound Hill, Crawley,
West Sussex RH10 3BA
Tel: 01293 882468
Real Ales, Bar Food, Restaurant Menu,
Disabled Facilities

164 The Three Crowns
10 Hammerwood Road, East Grinstead,
Sussex RH19 3TJ
Tel: 01342 410963
Real Ales, Bar Food, Restaurant Menu,
No Smoking Area, Disabled Facilities

165 Travellers-Fare
Crawley Railway Station Station Way, Crawley,
Sussex RH10 1JA
Tel: 01293 529138
Real Ales, Bar Food, Restaurant Menu,
Disabled Facilities

166 The Victory Inn
Warninglid Road, Haywards Heath,
Sussex RH17 6EU
Tel: 01444 400463
Real Ales, Bar Food, Restaurant Menu,
No Smoking Area

167 Watermill
1 Leylands Road, Worlds End, Burgess Hill,
Sussex RH15 0QF
Tel: 01444 235517
Real Ales, Bar Food, Disabled Facilities

168 Welcome Stranger
Crowborough Hill, Crowborough, Sussex TN6 2JL
Tel: 01892 655095
Real Ales, Bar Food, Disabled Facilities

169 The Wheatsheaf
Handcross Road, Plummers Plain, Horsham,
Sussex RH13 6NZ
Tel: 01444 400472
Real Ales, Bar Food, Restaurant Menu,
No Smoking Area, Disabled Facilities

170 The Wheatsheaf
Broad Street, Cuckfield, Haywards Heath,
Sussex RH17 5DW
Tel: 01444 454078
Real Ales, Bar Food, Restaurant Menu,
Accommodation, No Smoking Area, Disabled Facilities
See panel on page 54

170 The Wheatsheaf

Broad Street, Cuckfield, West Sussex RH17 5DW
☎ 01444 454078 ⊕ www.thewheatsheafpub.com

Real Ales, Bar Food, Restaurant Menu, Accommodation, No Smoking Area, Disabled Facilities

- ☛ Off the A272 2 miles W of Haywards Heath
- 🍺 Harveys, Flowers, Ringwood
- 🍴 12-2.30 & 6-9.30
- 🛏 10 rooms en suite
- 🎵 Quiz Thursday
- ⛏ Garden, car park
- 💳 Major cards accepted
- 🕐 12-11 (Sun to 10.30)
- 🏛 Haywards Heath 2 miles, Gatwick Airport 20mins (A23)

The Wheatsheaf is a place of many attractions – pub, hotel, fine dining restaurant and function venue. The outside of the building looks a picture in spring and summer, with a lovely display of flowers and shrubs, while the bars and dining areas combine tradition and style to delightful effect. Mine host is Marcus Pingriff. Harveys, Flowers and Ringwood brews keep connoisseurs of real ale happy, and diners can choose between a homestyle gastro bar menu and the superb Pingriffs Restaurant Seafood Restaurant, which is open every session except Sunday evening. The Wheatsheaf also excels on the accommodation side, and the 10 en suite bedrooms provide an excellent base for both leisure and business visitors.

173 The White Hart

Station Road, Buxted, Uckfield, Sussex TN22 4DP
☎ 01825 733192

Real Ales, Bar Food, Restaurant Menu, No Smoking Area, Disabled Facilities

- ☛ On the A272 2 miles NE of Uckfield
- 🍺 Badger first gold, Tanglefoot, K&B Sussex
- 🍴 12-2.30 & 6-9 (12-4 Sunday)
- ⛏ Patio, car park
- 💳 Major cards accepted
- 🕐 11.30-3 & 5.30-11 (all day Sat & Sun)
- 🏛 Sheffield Park NT 5 miles

On the A272 in the village of Buxted, the White Hart is a handsome redbrick Victorian pub that's equally popular with local residents, families, motorists taking a break and visitors to this attractive part of the county. This Hall and Woodhouse pub stocks a good selection of cask ales, beers, lagers, wines, spirits and soft drinks, and hosts Chris and Amy Bodsworth are expanding the food side of the business. In the bar, with its beams and big open fire, or in the bright conservatory restaurant, the menus provide ' pub grub with passion', from king prawns in filo pastry and crispy-coated camembert to cottage pie, beef & ale stew, ham, egg & chips, cod, plaice and stuffed chicken breast to much-loved desserts such as chocolate sponge or jam roly poly.

171 The White Hart

Chapel Green Lane, Crowborough,
Sussex TN6 2LB
Tel: 01892 652367

Real Ales, Bar Food, Restaurant Menu,
No Smoking Area, Disabled Facilities

172 White Hart

65 High Street, Crawley, Sussex RH10 1BQ
Tel: 01293 520033

Real Ales, Bar Food, Restaurant Menu,
Disabled Facilities

173 The White Hart

Station Road, Buxted, Uckfield, Sussex TN22 4DP
Tel: 01825 733192

Real Ales, Bar Food, Restaurant Menu,
No Smoking Area, Disabled Facilities

See panel opposite

174 White Hart Inn

Ardingly Road, West Hoathly, East Grinstead,
Sussex RH19 4RA
Tel: 01342 715217

Real Ales, Bar Food, Restaurant Menu,
No Smoking Area

175 The White Horse

22 High Street, Lindfield, Haywards Heath,
Sussex RH16 2HH
Tel: 01444 482251

Real Ales, Bar Food, Restaurant Menu,
No Smoking Area, Disabled Facilities

176 White Horse Inn

Park Lane, Maplehurst, Sussex RH13 6LL
Tel: 01403 891208

Real Ales, Bar Food, Restaurant Menu,
No Smoking Area, Disabled Facilities

184 Ye White Hart Inne

South Street, Cuckfield, West Sussex RH17 5LB
☎ 01444 413454

Real Ales, Bar Food, Restaurant Menu,
No Smoking Area

👉 From the end of the M23, follow the A23 south for 6 miles, then left onto the A272 following signs for Cuckfield

🍺 Sussex Best, Badger

🍴 12-2 Tues-Sun

🎵 Quiz Wed in summer, folk night last Sun of month

⛱ Beer garden, car park

💳 Major cards accepted

🕐 11.30-2.30 & 6-11 (Sun 7-10.30); closed Mon lunchtime

🏛 Borde Hill Gardens 2 miles, Nymans Gardens 2 miles, Bluebell Railway 5 miles

The handsome Victorian façade – the date '1881' flanks the pub sign – hides much earlier origins at **Ye White Hart Inne**, which has a strong classic appeal both inside and out. Tenants Jackie and Jim have made this a popular choice with both local residents and visitors, whether for a drink or for the value-for-money lunches served every day except Monday. Sussex Best and Badger ale head the list of beers, and the food choice includes classics such as half shoulder of lamb, chicken dishes and home-made curry. Open fires warm the intimate bar in the cooler months, and when the sun shines the place to be is the pretty sheltered garden adjoining the church, with fine views towards the South Downs. Wednesday is quiz night in the summer months, and the folk night on the last Sunday of the month always brings in the crowds.

177 The White Knight
Worth Road, Pound Hill, Crawley,
Sussex RH10 7DY
Tel: 01293 513197
Real Ales, Bar Food, Disabled Facilities

178 Whitehill Tavern
Whitehill Rd, Crowborough, East Sussex TN6 1JA
Tel: 01892 668786
Real Ales, Bar Food, No Smoking Area,
Disabled Facilities

179 The Windmill Inn
134 Leylands Road, Burgess Hill, Sussex RH15 8AB
Tel: 01444 235537
Bar Food

180 Windmill Inn
Littleworth Lane, Partridge Green, Horsham,
Sussex RH13 8EJ
Tel: 01403 710308
Real Ales, Bar Food

181 Wise Old Owl
Dorking Road, Kingsfold, Horsham,
Sussex RH12 3SA
Tel: 01306 628499
Real Ales, Bar Food, Restaurant Menu,
No Smoking Area, Disabled Facilities

182 The Woolpack
West St, Burgess Hill, West Sussex RH15 8NN
Tel: 01444 245178
Real Ales, Bar Food, Restaurant Menu,
No Smoking Area, Disabled Facilities

183 Ye Olde Stout House
29 Carfax, Horsham, Sussex RH12 1EE
Tel: 01403 267777
Real Ales

184 Ye White Hart Inne
South Street, Cuckfield, Haywards Heath,
Sussex RH17 5LB
Tel: 01444 413454
Real Ales, Bar Food, Restaurant Menu,
No Smoking Area
See panel on page 55

THE SUSSEX COAST – WORTHING TO NEWHAVEN

Brighton began life as a small fishing village but developed rapidly following Royal visits at the end of the 18th and beginning of the 19th century. The favoured resort of the Prince Regent is best known for the lavish Royal Pavilion, but it also has a particularly lively and cosmopolitan air, with a thriving leisure and cultural life. Inland, the major town is Lewes, with strong links to the Norman Conquest. In the classic Elizabethan mansion Danny, Lloyd George and his war cabinet drew up the terms of the armistice that ended the First World War.

Alfriston

In one of the oldest and best preserved villages in Sussex, the ancient market cross still stands in the square. Among the many interesting buildings is the thatched and timbered **Clergy House**, the first building acquired by the National Trust – in 1896 for £10.

Alfriston

Bramber

Bramber Castle, completed by William de Brose in 1040, was an important stronghold at a time when Bramber was still a port. It did not survive the Civil War, but the stark ruins can still be seen on a hilltop.

Brighton

Brighton was already becoming a popular place when the Prince Regent made his first visit in 1783, but he really made his mark with the **Royal Pavilion**, a modest farmhouse transformed by the architect Henry Holland and turned by John Nash into an Indian-inspired palace complete with minarets, pinnacles and onion domes. **The Lanes**, a warren of narrow streets surviving from the old village, is a place of boutiques, antique shops and eating houses.

Section 3

Burgess Hill
Henfield
Hurstpierpoint
Pyecombe
Steyning
Bramber
Upper Beeding
Poynings
Stanmer
Ringmer
Glyndebourne
Upper Dicker
Findon
Lewes
Beddingham
North Lancing
Brighton
Hove
Selmeston
Berwick
Wilmington
Shoreham
Rottingdean
Alfriston
Worthing
Goring-by-S
Peacehaven
Seaford
Newhaven
East Dean

Halland

Section 6

Section 2

▮▮ Pub or Inn Reference Number - Detailed Information

▮▮ Pub or Inn Reference Number - Summary Entry

● ▮ Place of interest mentioned in the chapter introduction

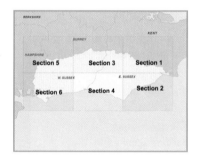

Section 5   Section 3   Section 1

Section 6   Section 4   Section 2

Brighton Marina

Hurstpierpoint

Dominating the countryside to the north is **Hurstpierpoint College Chapel**, while to the south stands the classic Elizabethan mansion **Danny**, where Lloyd George and his war cabinet drew up the terms of the armistice ending the First World War.

The best-known features on the seafront are the **Palace Pier** and the **Volk's Railway**, the first electric railway in the country.

Findon

An attractive village famous for its **Sheep Fair**, held every September since the 18th century. From Findon there is easy access to **Cissbury Ring**, the largest of the many Iron Age hill forts on the South Downs.

Glyndebourne

A mile north of Glynde village, **Glyndebourne** is a part-Tudor, part-Victorian country house where operas have been staged since 1934, when Mozart's *Marriage of Figaro* was performed.

Hove

Brighton's neighbour, famous for its Regency squares and broad, tree-lined avenues. Among the places of interest are the **Museum and Art Gallery** and the **British Engineerium** housed in a restored Victorian pumping station.

Lewes

The county town of East Sussex occupies a strategically important point where the River Ouse is crossed by an ancient east-west land route. William de Warenne, a friend of William the Conqueror, began the building of **Lewes Castle** and founded the great **Priory of St Pancras**. A substantial part of the castle still stands.

Newhaven

Newhaven Fort, built in the 19th century during one of the periodic French invasion scares, is today a museum with underground tunnels and galleries and a Home Front exhibition.

North Lancing

Lancing College, in a beautiful setting overlooking the River Adur, was founded in 1848 by Nathaniel Woodward with the aim of establishing a group of classless schools. The splendid Gothic chapel is the most striking of the College buildings.

The Gateway, Lewes

years the group known as the Bloomsbury Set regularly met here.

Shoreham

Places of interest here include two Norman churches, the halfmoon-shaped **Shoreham Fort** and **Marlipins Museum** housed in an ancient customs warehouse. Shoreham Airport (1934) is the country's oldest commercial airport.

Upper Dicker

In 1229, Augustinian canons chose this hamlet overlooking the River Cuckmere as the site for the beautiful **Michelham Priory**, which boasts England's longest water-filled medieval moat. In the Tudor mansion that evolved from the Priory, the rooms are graced with Dutch paintings, Flemish tapestries and old English furniture.

Poynings

Close by is one of the greatest natural features of the South Downs – the **Devil's Dyke**. This steep-sided ravine is a popular spot with tourists, walkers and hang-gliding enthusiasts.

Seaford

In the Martello Tower on the esplanade is the **Museum of Local History**, with artefacts and pictures of Seaford's history, collections of household and office equipment and tableaux of Victorian shops and homes.

Selmeston

The artist Vanessa Bell moved here to **Charleston Farmhouse** in 1916 with her art critic husband Clive and her lover Duncan Grant. Over the subsequent 50

Wilmington

Wilmington Priory was founded in the 11th century as an outpost of the Benedictine Abbey of Grestain in Normandy. Cut into the chalk of nearby Windover Hill is the famous **Long Man**, 253 feet long, with a 250ft shaft in each hand.

Worthing

The royal stamp of approval came to Worthing in 1798, when George III sent his daughter Princess Amelia here to rest her lame knee. It was here in 1894 that Oscar Wilde wrote *The Importance of Being Earnest* and immortalised its name in the central character Jack Worthing. **Worthing Museum** houses nationally important costume and toy collections.

1 Abergavenny Arms
Newhaven Road, Rodmell, Lewes, Sussex BN7 3EZ
Tel: 01273 472416
Real Ales, Bar Food, Restaurant Menu,
No Smoking Area

2 Albion Tavern
13-15 Fishersgate Terrace, Brighton,
Sussex BN41 1PH
Tel: 01273 411256
Real Ales

3 The Alexandra
28 Lyndhurst Road, Worthing, Sussex BN11 2DF
Tel: 01903 234833
Real Ales, Bar Food, Restaurant Menu,
No Smoking Area, Disabled Facilities

4 Anchor Inn
Anchor Lane, Barcombe, Lewes, Sussex BN8 5BS
Tel: 01273 400414
Real Ales, Bar Food, Restaurant Menu,
Accommodation, No Smoking Area, Disabled Facilities

5 The Anchor Inn
Lewes Road, Ringmer, Lewes, Sussex BN8 5QE
Tel: 01273 812370
Real Ales, Bar Food, Restaurant Menu,
No Smoking Area, Disabled Facilities

6 The Anchor Inn
46 High Street, Pulborough, Sussex RH20 4DU
Tel: 01903 742665
Real Ales, Bar Food, Restaurant Menu,
No Smoking Area, Disabled Facilities

7 The Ardington Hotel
Steyne Gardens, Worthing, Sussex BN11 3DZ
Tel: 01903 230451
Bar Food, Restaurant Menu, Accommodation,
Disabled Facilities

8 The Assembly
20 Chapel Road, Worthing, Sussex BN11 1BJ
Tel: 01903 204255
Bar Food

9 Badgers Watch
South Coast Road, Peacehaven, Sussex BN10 7BE
Tel: 01273 579031
Real Ales, Bar Food, Restaurant Menu,
No Smoking Area, Disabled Facilities

10 Balltree Inn
Busticle Lane, Sompting, Lancing,
Sussex BN15 0DH
Tel: 01903 753090
Real Ales, Bar Food, Restaurant Menu,
Disabled Facilities

11 Bar Breeze
42 Marine Parade, Worthing, Sussex BN11 3QA
Tel: 01903 232538

12 The Bay
Pelham Rd, Seaford, East Sussex BN25 1EP
Tel: 01323 873738
Real Ales, Bar Food, Restaurant Menu,
No Smoking Area

13 The Beach Comber
Dane Road, Seaford, Sussex BN25 1DX
Tel: 01323 892719
Real Ales, Bar Food, Restaurant Menu

14 Beach Hotel
Marine Parade, Worthing, Sussex BN11 3QJ
Tel: 01903 234001
Restaurant Menu, Accommodation, No Smoking Area,
Disabled Facilities

15 Berkeley Hotel
86-94 Marine Parade, Worthing, Sussex BN11
3QD
Tel: 01903 820000
Real Ales, Bar Food, Restaurant Menu,
Accommodation, No Smoking Area, Disabled Facilities

16 The Berwick Inn
Berwick, Polegate, Polegate, Sussex BN26 6SZ
Tel: 01323 871277
Real Ales, Bar Food, Restaurant Menu,
No Smoking Area

17 Birling Gap

Birling Gap, East Dean, Eastbourne,
Sussex BN20 0AB
Tel: 01323 423163

Real Ales, Bar Food, Restaurant Menu,
Accommodation, No Smoking Area, Disabled Facilities

18 Black Horse Inn

High Street, Findon, Worthing, Sussex BN14 0SX
Tel: 01903 872301

Real Ales, Bar Food, Restaurant Menu,
No Smoking Area, Disabled Facilities

19 Black Horse Inn

55 Western Road, Lewes, Sussex BN7 1RS
Tel: 01273 473653

Real Ales, Bar Food, Accommodation,
No Smoking Area

20 The Black Lion Inn

Lewes Rd, Halland, Lewes, East Sussex BN8 6PN
Tel: 01825 840304

Real Ales, Bar Food, Restaurant Menu,
Accommodation, No Smoking Area, Disabled Facilities

See panel below

21 Blacksmiths Arms

London Road, Offham, Lewes, Sussex BN7 3QD
Tel: 01273 472971

Real Ales, Bar Food, Restaurant Menu,
Accommodation, No Smoking Area, Disabled Facilities

22 The Blue Anchor

81 Station Road, Brighton, BN41 1DF
Tel: 01273 413064

Real Ales, Bar Food, Restaurant Menu,
Disabled Facilities

20 The Black Lion Inn

Lewes Road, Halland, East Sussex BN8 6PN
☎ 01825 840304

Real Ales, Bar Food, Restaurant Menu, Accommodation, No Smoking Area, Disabled Facilities

- The inn located on a roundabout at the junction of the A22 and B2192
- Harveys
- 12-2.30 & 6.30-9, all day Sunday
- 7 rooms (5 en suite)
- Patio, car park
- Major cards accepted
- 12-11
- Uckfield 5 miles, Hailsham 6 miles

Motorists will have no trouble in locating the **Black Lion Inn**, which stands on a busy roundabout where the A22 meets the B2192. With easy access to many places of interest both in the countryside and along the coast, this attractive tile-hung inn is an excellent base for a break, and the seven guest bedrooms (five with en suite facilities) ensure a very comfortable night's sleep. Food is an important and growing part of the business, and the Black Lion is doing a roaring trade in the hands of tenants John and Mandy, who have seen a big increase in custom since taking over in the spring of 2005. Bar snacks include filled baguettes and baked potatoes, and the main menu tempts with classics such as fish & chips (eat in or take away), cottage pie, liver & bacon, meat and vegetable curries and spaghetti with spicy meatballs, as well as more exotic specials such as peppered swordfish steak. The popular Sunday roasts are served all day.

23 The Bowl Inn
Brighton Road, Worthing, Sussex BN11 2DB
Tel: 01903 237722

Real Ales, Bar Food, Restaurant Menu,
No Smoking Area, Disabled Facilities

24 Brewers Arms
91 High Street, Lewes, Sussex BN7 1XN
Tel: 01273 475524

Real Ales, Bar Food, No Smoking Area

25 The Brewers Arms
251 London Road, Burgess Hill, Sussex RH15 9QU
Tel: 01444 232153

Real Ales, Bar Food

26 The Bridge
Bridge Street, Newhaven, Sussex BN9 9PH
Tel: 01273 514059

Real Ales, Bar Food, Accommodation,
Disabled Facilities

27 The Bridge Inn
87 High Street, Shoreham-By-Sea,
Sussex BN43 5DE
Tel: 01273 452477

Real Ales, Bar Food, Restaurant Menu,
Accommodation, Disabled Facilities

28 The Bridge Inn
High Street, Steyning, Sussex BN44 3HZ
Tel: 01903 812773

Real Ales, Bar Food, Restaurant Menu,
No Smoking Area

29 Broadwater
4 Broadwater Street West, Worthing,
Sussex BN14 9DA
Tel: 01903 238675

Real Ales, Bar Food, No Smoking Area,
Disabled Facilities

30 Buckingham Arms
Brunswick Road, Shoreham-By-Sea,
Sussex BN43 5WA
Tel: 01273 453660

Real Ales, Bar Food, Restaurant Menu

31 Bull Hotel
2 High Street, Ditchling, Hassocks, Sussex BN6 8TA
Tel: 01273 843147

Real Ales, Bar Food, Restaurant Menu,
Accommodation, No Smoking Area

32 The Bull Inn
London Road East, Henfield, Sussex BN5 9AD
Tel: 01273 492232

Real Ales, Bar Food, Restaurant Menu,
No Smoking Area, Disabled Facilities

33 Burlington Hotel
Marine Parade, Worthing, Sussex BN11 3QL
Tel: 01903 211222

Bar Food, Restaurant Menu, Accommodation,
No Smoking Area

34 Castle Hotel
The Street, Bramber, Steyning, Sussex BN44 3WE
Tel: 01903 812102

Real Ales, Bar Food, Restaurant Menu,
Accommodation, No Smoking Area, Disabled Facilities

35 Castle Tavern
1 Newland Road, Worthing, Sussex BN1 1JR
Tel: 01903 601000

Real Ales, Bar Food

36 Cavendish Hotel & Restaurant
115 Marine Parade, Worthing, Sussex BN11 3QG
Tel: 01903 236767

Real Ales, Bar Food, Restaurant Menu,
Accommodation

37 Chatsworth Hotel
17 23 The Steyne, Worthing, Sussex BN11 3DU
Tel: 01903 236103

Bar Food, Restaurant Menu, Accommodation,
No Smoking Area, Disabled Facilities

38 Chequer Inn
High Street, Steyning, Sussex BN44 3RE
Tel: 01903 814437

Real Ales, Bar Food, Restaurant Menu,
Accommodation, No Smoking Area

39 Cinque Ports
49 High Street, Seaford, Sussex BN25 1PP
Tel: 01323 892391
Real Ales, Bar Food, Restaurant Menu,
No Smoking Area, Disabled Facilities

40 The Clifton Arms
137 Clifton Road, Worthing, Sussex BN11 4DP
Tel: 01903 239527
Real Ales, Bar Food, Disabled Facilities

41 Coach & Horses
Arundel Road, Clapham, Worthing, Sussex BN13 3UA
Tel: 01903 264665
Real Ales, Bar Food, Restaurant Menu

42 Cock
Uckfield Road, Ringmer, Lewes, Sussex BN8 5RX
Tel: 01273 812040
Real Ales, Bar Food, Restaurant Menu,
No Smoking Area

43 The Crabtree
6 Buckingham Road, Shoreham-By-Sea,
Sussex BN43 5UA
Tel: 01273 463508
Accommodation, Disabled Facilities

44 The Crabtree Inn
140 Crabtree Lane, Lancing,
West Sussex BN15 9NQ
Tel: 01903 755514
Real Ales, Bar Food, No Smoking Area,
Disabled Facilities

45 The Cricketers
49 51 Church Road, Portslade, Brighton,
Sussex BN41 1LB
Tel: 01273 887888
No Smoking Area

46 The Cricketers
20 The Green, Southwick, Brighton,
Sussex BN42 4GF
Tel: 01273 592081
Real Ales, Bar Food, Restaurant Menu,
No Smoking Area, Disabled Facilities

47 The Cricketers
66 Broadwater Street West, Broadwater, Worthing,
Sussex BN14 9DE
Tel: 01903 233369
Real Ales, Bar Food, Restaurant Menu,
No Smoking Area, Disabled Facilities

48 Cricketers Arms
Polegate, Berwick, Sussex BN26 6SP
Tel: 01323 870469
Real Ales, Bar Food, Restaurant Menu,
No Smoking Area

49 Crown & Anchor
33 High Street, Shoreham-By-Sea,
Sussex BN43 5DD
Tel: 01273 452007
Real Ales, Bar Food, Restaurant Menu,
No Smoking Area

50 Crown Inn
High Street, Lewes, Sussex BN7 2NA
Tel: 01273 480670
Real Ales, Bar Food, Accommodation,
No Smoking Area

51 The Crown Inn
Worthing Road, Dial Post, Horsham,
Sussex RH13 8NH
Tel: 01403 710902
Real Ales, Bar Food, Restaurant Menu,
Accommodation, No Smoking Area

52 Crown Public House
12 Church Street, Seaford, Sussex BN25 1HG
Tel: 01323 891454
Real Ales, No Smoking Area

53 The Dorset Arms
22 Malling Street, Lewes, Sussex BN7 2RD
Tel: 01273 477110
Real Ales, Bar Food, Restaurant Menu,
No Smoking Area, Disabled Facilities

54 The Downview
1 Station Parade, Tarring, Worthing,
Sussex BN11 4SS
Tel: 01903 708791
Real Ales, Bar Food, Restaurant Menu,
No Smoking Area, Disabled Facilities

55 The Duke Of Wellington
368 Brighton Rd, Shoreham-By-Sea,
West Sussex BN43 6RE
Tel: 01273 389818
Real Ales

56 Duke Of York Inn
London Road, Sayers Common, Hassocks,
Sussex BN6 9HY
Tel: 01273 832262
Real Ales, Bar Food, Restaurant Menu,
Accommodation

57 Eden
58 Chapel Rd, Worthing, West Sussex BN11 1BN
Tel: 01903 823942
Bar Food, Restaurant Menu, Disabled Facilities

58 Egremont Hotel
Brighton Road, Worthing, Sussex BN11 3ED
Tel: 01903 201541
Real Ales, Accommodation, No Smoking Area,
Disabled Facilities

59 The Eight Bells
Polegate, Sussex BN26 5QB
Tel: 01323 484442
Real Ales, Bar Food, Restaurant Menu,
No Smoking Area

60 The Elms
66 Broadwater Street East, Broadwater, Worthing,
Sussex BN14 9AP
Tel: 01903 234130
Real Ales, Bar Food, No Smoking Area

61 The Engineer
76 Railway Road, Newhaven, Sussex BN9 0AY
Tel: 01273 514460
Real Ales, Bar Food

62 Farmers
17 South Street, Lancing, Sussex BN15 8AE
Tel: 01903 753097
Real Ales, Bar Food

63 Ferry Inn
1 East Street, Shoreham-By-Sea, Sussex BN43 5ZE
Tel: 01273 454125
Real Ales, Accommodation

64 Findon Manor
High Street, Findon, Worthing, Sussex BN14 0TA
Tel: 01903 872733
Real Ales, Bar Food, Restaurant Menu,
Accommodation, No Smoking Area

65 The Five Bells
Chailey Green, Lewes, Sussex BN8 4DA
Tel: 01825 722259
Real Ales, Bar Food, Restaurant Menu,
No Smoking Area, Disabled Facilities

66 The Flying Fish
42 Denton Road, Newhaven, Sussex BN9 0QB
Tel: 01273 515440
Real Ales, Bar Food, Restaurant Menu,
Accommodation, No Smoking Area, Disabled Facilities

67 The Foresters Arms
6 South Street, East Hoathly, Lewes, Sussex BN8 6DS
Tel: 01825 840208
Real Ales, Bar Food, Restaurant Menu,
No Smoking Area, Disabled Facilities

68 The Fountain Inn
Station Road, Plumpton Green, Lewes,
Sussex BN7 3BX
Tel: 01273 890294
Real Ales, Bar Food, Restaurant Menu,
Accommodation, Disabled Facilities
See panel on page 66

69 Fountain Inn
Horsham Road, Ashurst, Steyning,
Sussex BN44 3AP
Tel: 01403 710219
Real Ales, Bar Food, Restaurant Menu,
Disabled Facilities

68 The Fountain Inn

Station Road, Plumpton Green, Lewes,
East Sussex BN7 3BX
☎ 01273 890294
e-mail: thefountaininn@btconnect.com

**Real Ales, Bar Food, Restaurant Menu,
Accommodation, Disabled Facilities**

- ☛ Close to the A275 very close to Plumpton Racecourse
- 🍺 Young's Bitter, Ramrod
- 🍴 12-2.30 & 6-9.30 (snacks all day)
- 🛏 2 rooms
- 🎵 Quiz last Saturday of month, computer wireless connection
- ⚓ Patio
- 💳 Major cards accepted
- 🕐 11-4 & 6-12
- 🏛 Plumpton races short walk, plus walks on downs

The Fountain Inn near the railway station in the village of Plumpton Green, easily reached from the A275 north of Lewes. The inn is a short walk from Plumpton's National

Hunt racecourse, and many racegoers seek out the Fountain before or after a day's racing. When it comes to traditional hospitality, everyone's a winner at this splendid pub, where Teresa Bradford and her family provide a selection of snacks in addition to the main menu served every lunchtime and evening (a la carte). Sausage & mash, chilli prawns, shepherd's pie and steaks are among the favourites, and Wednesday is curry night, with a choice of Madras, Masala and Korma. Computer wireless connection allow visitors to log on over a pint, and for punters wanting an early start or a late celebration the pub has two rooms for B&B.

70 The Fox

Henfield Rd, Small Dole, Henfield,
West Sussex BN5 9XE
Tel: 01273 491196

Real Ales, Bar Food, Restaurant Menu,
No Smoking Area, Disabled Facilities

71 The Frankland Arms

London Road Business Park, Washington,
Pulborough, Sussex RH20 4AL
Tel: 01903 892220

Real Ales, Bar Food, Restaurant Menu,
No Smoking Area, Disabled Facilities

72 Gardeners Arms

Nep Town Road, Henfield, Sussex BN5 9DU
Tel: 01273 492411

Real Ales

73 The Gardeners Arms

West St, Sompting, Lancing,
West Sussex BN15 0AR
Tel: 01903 233666

Real Ales, Bar Food, Restaurant Menu,
No Smoking Area, Disabled Facilities

74 Gardeners Arms & Sidings Restaurant

West Street, Sompting, Lancing, Sussex BN11 3PT
Tel: 01903 526416

Real Ales, Bar Food, Restaurant Menu,
No Smoking Area, Disabled Facilities

75 George Inn

High Street, Alfriston, Polegate, Sussex BN26 5SY
Tel: 01323 870319

Real Ales, Bar Food, Restaurant Menu,
Accommodation, No Smoking Area

76 Giants Rest

The Street, Wilmington, Polegate, Sussex BN26 5SQ
Tel: 01323 870207

Real Ales, Bar Food, Restaurant Menu,
No Smoking Area, Disabled Facilities

77 Golden Cross Inn

Golden Cross, Hailsham, East Sussex BN27 4AW
Tel: 01825 872216

Real Ales, Bar Food, Restaurant Menu,
No Smoking Area, Disabled Facilities

78 Golden Galleon

Exceat Bridge, Seaford, Sussex BN25 4AB
Tel: 01323 892247

Real Ales, Restaurant Menu, No Smoking Area,
Disabled Facilities

79 The Golden Lion

7 The Strand, Worthing, Sussex BN12 6DL
Tel: 01903 245439

Real Ales, Bar Food, Restaurant Menu

80 Grand Victorian Hotel

27 Railway Approach, Worthing, Sussex BN11 1UR
Tel: 01903 230690

Real Ales, Bar Food, Restaurant Menu,
Accommodation, No Smoking Area, Disabled Facilities

81 The Green Man

Lewes Road, Lewes, Sussex BN8 5NA
Tel: 01273 812422

Real Ales, Bar Food, Restaurant Menu,
No Smoking Area, Disabled Facilities

82 Gullens

67 Longridge Avenue, Saltdean, Brighton,
Sussex BN2 8LG
Tel: 01273 302564

Bar Food, Restaurant Menu

83 **The Gun at Findon**

High Street, Findon, Worthing, Sussex BN14 0TA
Tel: **01903 873206**

Real Ales, Bar Food, Restaurant Menu,
No Smoking Area

See panel below

83 **The Gun at Findon**

High STreet, Findon, West Sussex BN14 0TA
☎ 01903 873206

**Real Ales, Bar Food, Restaurant Menu,
No Smoking Area**

☛   In the centre of Findon, off the A24 3 miles N
     of Worthing

🍺   Adnams, Broadside, London Pride, Harveys

🍴   Lunchtime & Evening, snacks all day

⛏   Garden with picnic benches, off-road parking

💳   Major cards accepted

🕐   All day

🏛   South Downs on doorstep; Worthing 3 miles

The Gun at Findon has a long and interesting history that can be traced back at least to the 15th century. In the 1700s it became an important stopping point for coaches, and was referred to as 'a good inn' in a directory of such places - the 'Country Inns & Pubs' of its day, no doubt. Heavy black beams

and old panelling create the perfect ambience for relaxing with a drink, but the Gun is also one of the very best eating places for miles around. The menus tempt with choices that run from classics like pork & sage sausages with mash and onion gravy to specials such as chicken and red pepper terrine with gooseberry chutney, sea bass fillets with a fennel and watercress sauce or, for vegetarians, oven-roasted ratatouille and mozzarella strudel. A separate bar snack menu is also available.

84 The Gun Inn

Gun Hill, Heathfield, Sussex TN21 0JU
Tel: 01825 872361

Real Ales, Bar Food, Restaurant Menu,
No Smoking Area

85 Half Moon Inn

Lewes Road, Plumpton, Lewes, Sussex BN7 3AF
Tel: 01273 890253

Real Ales, Bar Food, No Smoking Area

86 Halland Forge Hotel

Halland, Lewes, Sussex BN8 6PW
Tel: 01825 840456

Bar Food, Restaurant Menu, Accommodation,
No Smoking Area, Disabled Facilities

87 Hampden Arms

Heighton Road, South Heighton, Newhaven,
Sussex BN9 0JJ
Tel: 01273 514529

Real Ales

88 The Harbour View

35 Wellington Road, Portslade, Brighton,
Sussex BN41 1DN
Tel: 01273 413019

Real Ales, Disabled Facilities

89 The Harbourside

Fort Rd, Newhaven, East Sussex BN9 9EL
Tel: 01273 513340

Real Ales, Bar Food, Restaurant Menu,
Accommodation, No Smoking Area, Disabled Facilities

90 Hare & Hounds

79-81 Portland Road, Worthing, Sussex BN11 1QG
Tel: 01903 230085

Real Ales, Bar Food, Restaurant Menu,
No Smoking Area

91 Harvey's

20 Southwick Square, Brighton, Sussex BN42 4FJ
Tel: 01273 870461

Restaurant Menu, No Smoking Area

92 The Hassocks

Station Approach East, Hassocks, Sussex BN6 8HN
Tel: 01273 842113

Real Ales, Bar Food, Restaurant Menu,
No Smoking Area, Disabled Facilities

93 Henfield Tavern

High Street, Henfield, Sussex BN5 9HN
Tel: 01273 494534

Real Ales, Bar Food, Restaurant Menu,
Accommodation, Disabled Facilities

94 Horam Inn

High Street, Horam, Heathfield, Sussex TN21 0EL
Tel: 01435 812692

Real Ales, Bar Food, Restaurant Menu,
Accommodation, No Smoking Area

95 Horns Lodge

South Street, South Chailey, Lewes, Sussex BN8 4BD
Tel: 01273 400422

Real Ales, Bar Food, Restaurant Menu,
No Smoking Area, Disabled Facilities

96 Inn On The Park

Deanland Wood Park, Hailsham, Sussex BN27 3RN
Tel: 01825 872406

Real Ales, Bar Food, Restaurant Menu,
No Smoking Area, Disabled Facilities

97 J B'S Bar

New Street, Worthing, Sussex BN11 3BT
Tel: 01903 821530

Real Ales

98 Jack & Jill Inn

Brighton Road, Clayton, Hassocks, Sussex BN6 9PD
Tel: 01273 843595

Real Ales, Bar Food, Restaurant Menu,
Accommodation, No Smoking Area, Disabled Facilities

99 John Henry's

Nepcote Lane, Findon Village, Worthing,
West Sussex BN14 0SE
Tel: 01903 877277

Real Ales, Bar Food, Restaurant Menu,
Accommodation, No Smoking Area

100 The John Selden

Halfmoon Lane, Salvington, Worthing,
Sussex BN13 2HN
Tel: 01903 264986

Real Ales, Bar Food, Restaurant Menu,
No Smoking Area

101 The Jolly Boatman

133-135 Lewes Road, Newhaven, Sussex BN9 9SJ
Tel: 01273 510030

Real Ales

102 The Jolly Brewers

39-41 Clifton Road, Worthing, Sussex BN11 4DG
Tel: 01903 200060

Real Ales, Bar Food, Disabled Facilities

103 Jolly Sportsman

Chapel Lane, East Chiltington, Sussex BN7 3BA
Tel: 01273 890400

Real Ales, Bar Food, Restaurant Menu,
No Smoking Area, Disabled Facilities

104 The Juggs Arms

The Street, Kingston, Lewes, Sussex BN7 3NT
Tel: 01273 472523

Real Ales, Bar Food, Restaurant Menu,
No Smoking Area, Disabled Facilities

105 The Kings Head

Fishersgate Terrace, Portslade, Brighton,
Sussex BN41 1PH
Tel: 01273 422908

Real Ales, Bar Food, Accommodation,
No Smoking Area

106 The Kings Head

9 Southover High Street, Lewes, Sussex BN7 1HS
Tel: 01273 474628

Real Ales, Bar Food, Restaurant Menu,
Accommodation, No Smoking Area

107 The Kings Head

Lower Horsebridge, , Sussex BN27 4DL
Tel: 01323 843712

Real Ales, Bar Food, Restaurant Menu,
Accommodation, No Smoking Area, Disabled Facilities

108 The Kings Head Inn

High Street, Upper Beeding, Steyning,
Sussex BN44 3HZ
Tel: 01903 812196

Real Ales, Bar Food, Restaurant Menu,
No Smoking Area, Disabled Facilities

109 Kings Head Inn

London Road, Burgess Hill, Sussex RH15 8NB
Tel: 01444 232185

Real Ales, Bar Food, Restaurant Menu,
No Smoking Area, Disabled Facilities

110 Kingsway Hotel

117 Marine Parade, Worthing, Sussex BN11 3QQ
Tel: 01903 237542

Real Ales, Bar Food, Restaurant Menu,
Accommodation, No Smoking Area, Disabled Facilities

111 The Lamb

10 Fisher St, Lewes, East Sussex BN7 2DG
Tel: 01273 470950

Real Ales, Bar Food, Restaurant Menu,
Disabled Facilities

112 Lamb Inn

Church Lane, Ripe, Lewes, Sussex BN8 6AS
Tel: 01323 811280

Real Ales, Bar Food, Restaurant Menu,
No Smoking Area, Disabled Facilities

113 The Lamb Inn

Salvington Road, Durrington, Worthing,
Sussex BN13 2JR
Tel: 01903 263356

Real Ales, Bar Food, Restaurant Menu,
No Smoking Area, Disabled Facilities

See panel on page 70

114 The Lansdown Arms

36 Lansdown Place East, Lewes, Sussex BN7 2JU
Tel: 01273 480623

Real Ales

113 The Lamb Inn

Salvington Road, Durrington, nr Worthing,
West Sussex BN13 2JR
☎ 01903 263356

🌐 www.thelambdurrington.co.uk

Real Ales, Bar Food, Restaurant Menu,
No Smoking Area, Disabled Facilities

☛ Just off the A27 on the northwestern edge of
Worthing

🍺 3 rotating (1 from a local microbrewery)

🍴 12-2 & 5-9 (all day Sat & Sun)

🎵 Live music Thursday

🎪 Garden with children's play area, BBQ terrace

💳 Major cards except Amex and Diners

🕐 All day every day

🏛 Worthing 1 mile, High Salvington Windmill 1
mile, Findon (Cissbury Ring) 3 miles

Just off the A27 on the northwestern fringes
of Worthing, the **Lamb Inn** attracts a broad
cross-section of locals, motorists and
holidaymakers. David Hill has a warm
welcome for visitors of all ages, ably assisted by
cheerful, hardworking bar staff Gareth and Jay.
There's good disabled access, baby changing
facilities and a play area in the garden
complete with a bouncy castle in summer.
Regular summer barbecues supplement a fine
year-round choice of home-cooked dishes that
make excellent use of local produce.

115 Laughing Fish

Station Road, Isfield, Uckfield, Sussex TN22 5XB
Tel: 01825 750349

Real Ales, Bar Food, Restaurant Menu,
No Smoking Area

116 Lewes Arms

Mount Place, Lewes, Sussex BN7 1YH
Tel: 01273 473152

Real Ales, Bar Food, Restaurant Menu

117 The Light Bar

31 Chatsworth Road, Worthing, Sussex BN11 1LY
Tel: 01903 235284

Real Ales, Disabled Facilities

118 Marine View Hotel

111 Marine Parade, Worthing, Sussex BN11 3QG
Tel: 01903 238413

Bar Food, Restaurant Menu, Accommodation

119 Marlipins

38 High Street, Shoreham-By-Sea,
Sussex BN43 5DA
Tel: 01273 453369

Bar Food, Restaurant Menu, No Smoking Area,
Disabled Facilities

120 The Marquis Of Granby

1 West Street, Sompting, Lancing,
Sussex BN15 0AP
Tel: 01903 231102

Real Ales, Bar Food, Restaurant Menu,
No Smoking Area, Disabled Facilities

121 The May Garland Inn

Heathfield, Sussex TN21 0LJ
Tel: 01435 812249

Real Ales, Bar Food, Restaurant Menu

122 Mayfair Hotel

11-12 Heene Terrace, Worthing, Sussex BN11 3NS
Tel: 01903 201943

Real Ales, Bar Food, Restaurant Menu,
Accommodation, No Smoking Area

123 The Merry Monk

1 North Road, Lancing, Sussex BN15 9AH
Tel: 01903 764215

Real Ales, Bar Food, Restaurant Menu

124 The Montague Arms

149 Montague Street, Worthing, Sussex BN11 3BX
Tel: 01903 202419

Real Ales, Bar Food, Restaurant Menu

125 The Mulberry

Goring Road, Worthing, Sussex BN12 4NX
Tel: 01903 241555

Real Ales, Bar Food, Restaurant Menu,
No Smoking Area, Disabled Facilities

126 The Newfield Arms
69 Brighton Road, Newhaven,
Sussex BN9 9NG
Tel: 01273 513841
Real Ales

127 The Norfolk Arms
18 Church Street, Steyning, Sussex BN44 3YB
Tel: 01903 812215
Real Ales

128 The North Star
Littlehampton Road, Worthing, Sussex BN13 1QY
Tel: 01903 247973
Real Ales, Bar Food, No Smoking Area,
Disabled Facilities

129 The Old Boot Inn
16 South St, Seaford, East Sussex BN25 1PE
Tel: 01323 895454
Real Ales, Bar Food, Restaurant Menu,
No Smoking Area, Disabled Facilities

130 Old Oak Inn
Caneheath, Arlington, Nr Polegate, Sussex BN26 6SJ
Tel: 01323 482072
Real Ales, Bar Food, Restaurant Menu,
No Smoking Area, Disabled Facilities

131 The Old Plough
20 Church Street, Seaford, Sussex BN25 1HG
Tel: 01323 872921
Real Ales, No Smoking Area, Disabled Facilities

132 The Old Ship
Uckfield Rd, Ringmer, East Sussex BN8 5RP
Tel: 01273 814223
Real Ales, Restaurant Menu, No Smoking Area
See panel below

133 The Old Tollgate Restaurant & Hotel
The Street, Steyning, Sussex BN44 3WE
Tel: 01903 815104
Real Ales, Restaurant Menu, Accommodation,
No Smoking Area, Disabled Facilities

132 The Old Ship
Uckfield Road, Ringmer, East Sussex BN8 5RP
☎ 01273 814223

Real Ales, Restaurant Menu, No Smoking Area

 Ringmer is located on the B2192, off the A26
3 miles east of Lewes

 Sussex Best

 12-9.30

 Garden, car park

 Major cards accepted

🕐 11-11

🏛 Lewes 3 miles, Bentley Wildfowl & Motor Museum 2 miles

Michael Burdass heads the family team who run this lovely old country pub just outside the village of Ringmer, one of the oldest settlements in Sussex. The Old Ship dates back to the early 17th century and served what was once an important coaching route. The customers nowadays come from near and far to enjoy the fine hospitality and the excellent choice of home-cooked dishes, all prepared in house from the freshest produce. The regular menu is supplemented by a long list of daily specials which include super pies (fish, chicken & bacon, lamb & apricot), and lovely dishes like lemon sole with tarragon butter, or ribeye steak with a creamy stilton sauce. The bar and restaurant have a delightfully traditional look, and in summer the large garden is a pleasant spot for taking the air while enjoying a drink.

134 The Partridge

Church Road, Partridge Green, Horsham,
Sussex RH13 8JS
Tel: 01403 710391
Real Ales, Bar Food, Restaurant Menu,
No Smoking Area, Disabled Facilities

135 Pelham Arms

High Street, Lewes, Sussex BN7 1XL
Tel: 01273 476149
Real Ales, Bar Food, Restaurant Menu,
No Smoking Area

136 The Pilot

Southwick Railway Station Station Road, Brighton,
Sussex BN42 4AE
Tel: 01273 591789
Real Ales, Bar Food, Restaurant Menu,
No Smoking Area

137 The Plough

High Street, Henfield, Sussex BN5 9HP
Tel: 01273 492280
Real Ales, Bar Food, Restaurant Menu,
No Smoking Area
See panel below

138 Plough & Harrow

The Street, Litlington, Sussex BN26 5RN
Tel: 01323 870632
Real Ales, Bar Food, No Smoking Area

139 Plough Inn

London Road East, Pyecombe, Brighton,
Sussex BN45 7FN
Tel: 01273 842796
Real Ales, Bar Food, Restaurant Menu,
Accommodation, No Smoking Area, Disabled Facilities

137 The Plough

High Street, Henfield, East Sussex BN5 9HP
☎ 01273 492280

Real Ales, Bar Food, Restaurant Menu,
No Smoking Area

- On the main street of Henfield, on the A281 halfway between Horsham and Shoreham
- Harveys Sussex Best, London Pride, Horsham Best, Boddingtons.
- 12-9.30
- Beer garden
- Major cards accepted
- 11-11 (Sun 12-10.30)
- Hickstead 3 miles, South Downs Way 3 miles, Devil's Dyke 5 miles, Shoreham-by-Sea 7 miles

Anthony and Shirley Smith run the **Plough**, an old coaching inn in a village that was once a major staging post. Henfield has a fine Saxon church, a museum and several interesting old buildings, but for visitors in search of the traditional qualities of a country pub the Plough is the centre of attraction. This early-18th century building is easy to spot on the main street with its floral displays, ornate terracotta tiles and an old ploughshare above the entrance. In the bar, a wide variety of real ales are on tap, along with wines by the glass (two sizes) to enjoy over a chat or to accompany the excellent home cooking. The food choice, served all day, runs from tapas-style light bites (white asparagus with lemon mayonnaise) to fresh fish specials, chicken breast with garlic and basil, and a hearty steak & ale pie.

140 The Plough Inn

Station Road, Plumpton Green, Lewes,
Sussex BN7 3DF
Tel: 01273 890311
Real Ales, Bar Food, Restaurant Menu,
No Smoking Area

141 The Poacher

139 High St, Hurstpierpoint, Hassocks,
West Sussex BN6 9PU
Tel: 01273 834202
Real Ales, Bar Food

142 The Potters Arms

129 Station Road, Burgess Hill, Sussex RH15 9ED
Tel: 01444 233448
Real Ales, Bar Food, No Smoking Area

143 Pumphouse

Main Road, Cooksbridge, Lewes, Sussex BN8 4SW
Tel: 01273 400528
Real Ales, Bar Food, Restaurant Menu,
Accommodation, No Smoking Area

144 Railway Tavern

Upper Station Road, Henfield, Sussex BN5 9PJ
Tel: 01273 492509
Real Ales, Bar Food, Restaurant Menu,
No Smoking Area

145 **The Rainbow**

179 High Street, Lewes, Sussex BN7 1YE
Tel: 01273 472170
Real Ales, Bar Food, No Smoking Area
See panel below

---

145 **The Rainbow**

179 High Street, Lewes, East Sussex BN7 1YE
☎ 01273 472170   🌐 www.therainbow.lewes.co.uk

Real Ales, Bar Food, No Smoking Area

- On the main street of Lewes
- Harveys
- 12-3 & 5-8
- Occasional quiz nights and 'open mike' nights
- Roof terrace
- Major cards accepted
- 12-10.30 (Sun 12-4)
- Lewes Castle, museums, Anne of Cleves House; Brighton 7 miles

On the main street of Lewes, the Rainbow is a cheerful town pub that combines the traditional qualities of hospitality with a bright, up-to-date appearance. Behind the flower-decked redbrick and sandstone frontage the bar and dining areas have an uncluttered contemporary look and a combination of neat modern tables and chairs and some squishy leather sofas. Natasha and her staff provide a particularly interesting choice of food lunchtime and evening. Everything is cooked on the premises – they even bake their own bread – and dishes on the menu and specials board show a skilled, imaginative hand in the kitchen. peach, parma ham and blue cheese toasted ciabatta, slow-roasted pork, red pepper and coconut curry, roast sweet potato, walnut and parmesan salad, mixed berry pavlova with passion fruit ice cream. Lots of draught and bottled beers, lagers, wines, cocktails and shots are available all day.

146 The Ram Inn

The Street, Firle, East Sussex BN8 6NS

☎ 01273 858222 ⊕ www.theram-inn.com

Real Ales, Bar Food, Restaurant Menu,
No Smoking Area, Disabled Facilities

☛ From the A27 4 miles beyond Lewes, Firle is signposted past the turning for the A26

🍺 Harveys + guests

🍴 12-3 & 6.30-9.30 (Sat 12-9.30, Sun 12-6) no food Mon eve in winter

🅿 Car park, garden

💳 Major cards accepted

🕐 11.30-11 (Sun 12-10.30)

🏛 Firle Place 1 mile, Glyndebourne 3 miles, Lewes Castle 5 miles

In a quiet, tree-lined lane in the tranquil village of Firle, the Ram Inn is a popular destination for a wide cross-section of visitors of all ages. The redbrick building was once the local law

court, complete with a cell for holding prisoners awaiting trial, and to this day there are many reminders of its 16th century origins.

The bar, snug and family room are particularly warm and inviting, with log fires, sturdy furniture and lots of cosy corners, while outside is a delightful walled garden where a marquee can be made available in the summer months. Licensees Shaun and Hayley are rightly proud of the food served here every lunchtime and evening and all day on Saturday and Sunday; they believe in taste, freshness and quality, so all the dishes, including sauces and puddings, are made freshly on the premises on a daily basis from the best-quality locally sourced produce.

Some of the ingredients come from smaller farms that can guarantee the required quality, with produce raised or grown in an environmentally friendly way. The sandwiches – try smoked chicken breast with parma ham topped with tarragon mayonnaise on focaccia with salad and string fries! – are meals in themselves, while typical dishes elsewhere on the menu include cod, prawn and chive fish cakes (starter or main course), homemade minted lamb burgers, grilled fillet of salmon on a rich shrimp chowder and chicken, leek and smoky bacon puff pastry pie. Desserts like sticky toffee pudding or lemon tart with pistachio cream keep the enjoyment level high to the very end. Children can be served half-portions of most dishes on the menu.

Harveys Bitter is the resident real ale, and there are always two guest ales and a hand-pulled cider. This outstanding inn lies off the A27 4 miles east of Lewes at the foot of the South Downs – the South Downs Way is just a mile away.

146 The Ram Inn

The Street, Firle, Lewes, Sussex BN8 6NS
Tel: 01273 858222

Real Ales, Bar Food, Restaurant Menu,
No Smoking Area, Disabled Facilities

See panel opposite

147 The Red Lion

London Road, Ashington, Pulborough,
Sussex RH20 3DD
Tel: 01903 892226

Real Ales, Bar Food, Restaurant Menu,
No Smoking Area, Disabled Facilities

148 Red Lion Inn

Old Shoreham Road, Shoreham-By-Sea,
Sussex BN43 5TE
Tel: 01273 453171

Real Ales, Bar Food, Restaurant Menu,
No Smoking Area

149 The Rest

5 Bath Place, Worthing, West Sussex BN11 3BA
Tel: 01903 216032

150 Richard Cobden

2 Cobden Road, Worthing, Sussex BN11 4BD
Tel: 01903 236856

Real Ales, Bar Food

151 The Rising Sun

Shoreham Road, Steyning, Sussex BN44 3TN
Tel: 01903 814424

Real Ales, Bar Food, Restaurant Menu,
Accommodation, No Smoking Area

152 The Romans

Manor Hall Rd, Southwick, Brighton,
East Sussex BN42 4NG
Tel: 01273 592147

Real Ales, Bar Food, No Smoking Area,
Disabled Facilities

153 The Rose & Crown

169 173 Montague Street, Worthing,
Sussex BN11 3DA
Tel: 01903 201623

Real Ales, Bar Food, Restaurant Menu,
No Smoking Area

154 Rose Cottage Inn

Alciston, Polegate, Sussex BN26 6UW
Tel: 01323 870377

Real Ales, Bar Food, Restaurant Menu,
Accommodation, No Smoking Area

155 The Royal Coach

Brighton Road, Shoreham-By-Sea, Sussex BN43 5LD
Tel: 01273 454077

Real Ales, Bar Food, Restaurant Menu,
No Smoking Area, Disabled Facilities

156 Royal George

Upper Shoreham Road, Shoreham-By-Sea,
Sussex BN43 6TA
Tel: 01273 591904

Real Ales, Bar Food, Restaurant Menu,
No Smoking Area, Disabled Facilities

157 Royal Oak

High Street, Barcombe, Lewes, Sussex BN8 5BA
Tel: 01273 400418

Real Ales, Bar Food, Restaurant Menu,
No Smoking Area, Disabled Facilities

158 The Royal Oak

3 Station Street, Lewes, Sussex BN7 2DA
Tel: 01273 474803

Real Ales, Bar Food, Restaurant Menu

159 The Royal Oak

67 Brighton Road, Worthing, Sussex BN11 3EE
Tel: 01903 238888

Real Ales, Bar Food, Restaurant Menu,
No Smoking Area

161 The Royal Sovereign

Middle Street, Shoreham-by-Sea,
East Sussex BN43 5DP

☎ 01273 453518

Real Ales, Bar Food

- In a lane off the main street of Shoreham
- Large selection
- 12.30-2.30, also Wed 6-9, Sun 9.30-4
- Car park
- Major cards accepted
- 11-11 (Sun 9.30am -10.30pm)
- Worthing 4 miles, Brighton 5 miles

In a little lane off the main street in historic Shoreham-by-Sea, the **Royal Sovereign** has earned a lofty reputation as a place of great character and wide appeal. The building dates from the early 18th century, and behind the flower-decked, green-tiled frontage, the bars and dining areas boast many interesting features, including a handsome fireplace (more tiles here), leaded coloured glass on ceiling-height beams, a wood-panelled bar counter and a series of caricature prints. Food is big business here, and besides the extensive regular menu the pub serves Sunday breakfast from 9.30 to 11.30. Traditional Sunday roasts take over from 12 to 4, and Wednesday is curry night, when a generous serving of curry comes at a bargain all-in price with a pint of beer or a glass of wine.

---

160 The Royal Oak

The Street, Brighton, Sussex BN45 7AQ
Tel: 01273 857389
Real Ales, Bar Food, Restaurant Menu,
No Smoking Area

161 The Royal Sovereign

6 Middle Street, Shoreham-By-Sea,
Sussex BN43 5DP
Tel: 01273 453518

Real Ales, Bar Food

See panel above

162 Sarumdale Ltd

102 London Rd, Burgess Hill,
West Sussex RH15 8NB
Tel: 01444 243573
Real Ales, Bar Food, No Smoking Area,
Disabled Facilities

163 The Schooner

Albion Street, Brighton, Sussex BN42 4AU
Tel: 01273 592252
Real Ales, Bar Food, Restaurant Menu,
No Smoking Area

164 The Seven Sisters

Alfriston Road, Seaford, Sussex BN25 3PY
Tel: 01323 896548
Real Ales, Bar Food, Restaurant Menu

165 Shaves Thatch

Albourne, Hassocks, Sussex BN6 9EA
Tel: 01273 857324
Real Ales, Bar Food, Restaurant Menu,
No Smoking Area, Disabled Facilities

166 The Ship Inn

Southwick Street, Brighton, Sussex BN42 4AD
Tel: 01273 592958
Real Ales, Bar Food

167 The Shore Hotel
7 Dane Road, Seaford, Sussex BN25 ILG
Tel: 01323 896719

Real Ales, Bar Food, Restaurant Menu,
No Smoking Area, Disabled Facilities

168 The Sir Timothy Shelley
47-49 Chapel Rd, Worthing,
West Sussex BN11 IEG
Tel: 01903 228070

Real Ales, Bar Food, Restaurant Menu,
No Smoking Area, Disabled Facilities

169 Six Bells Inn
Chiddingly, Lewes, Sussex BN8 6HE
Tel: 01825 872227

Real Ales, Bar Food, Restaurant Menu,
No Smoking Area, Disabled Facilities

170 The Smugglers Return
112 Ham Rd, Worthing, West Sussex BN11 2QS
Tel: 01903 233146

Real Ales, Bar Food, Disabled Facilities

171 Snowdrop Inn
South Street, Lewes, Sussex BN7 2BU
Tel: 01273 471018

Real Ales, Bar Food, Restaurant Menu,
No Smoking Area

172 The Spanish Lady
4-6 Longridge Avenue, Brighton, Sussex BN2 8LH
Tel: 01273 303383

Real Ales, Bar Food, No Smoking Area

173 Springwells Hotel
High Street, Steyning, Sussex BN44 3GG
Tel: 01903 812043

Accommodation, No Smoking Area

174 The Stags Head
37 High Street, Portslade, Brighton,
Sussex BN41 2LH
Tel: 01273 417337

Real Ales

175 Stanley Arms
47 Wolseley Road, Portslade, Sussex BN41 ISS
Tel: 01273 430234

Real Ales

176 Star Inn
130 High Street, Steyning, Sussex BN44 3RD
Tel: 01903 813078

Real Ales, Bar Food, No Smoking Area

177 Star Inn
Waldron, Heathfield, Sussex TN21 0RA
Tel: 01435 812495

Real Ales, Bar Food, Restaurant Menu,
No Smoking Area, Disabled Facilities

178 The Sussex Coaster
82 South Coast Rd, Peacehaven,
East Sussex BN10 8SJ
Tel: 01273 582145

Real Ales, Bar Food, Accommodation,
Disabled Facilities

179 Sussex Ox
Milton Street, Alfriston, Polegate,
Sussex BN26 5RL
Tel: 01323 870840

Real Ales, Bar Food, Restaurant Menu,
No Smoking Area

180 Swan Inn
79 High Street, Worthing, Sussex BN11 IDN
Tel: 01903 232923

Real Ales, Bar Food, Restaurant Menu

181 The Swan Inn
30A Southover High Street, Lewes, Sussex BN7 IHU
Tel: 01273 480211

Real Ales, Bar Food

182 The Swiss Cottage
34 Old Shoreham Rd, Shoreham-By-Sea,
West Sussex BN43 5TD
Tel: 01273 453301

Real Ales, Bar Food, No Smoking Area

183 Tally Ho
Baxter Road, Lewes, Sussex BN7 2SP
Tel: 01273 474759
Real Ales, Bar Food, Disabled Facilities

184 Telscombe Tavern
405 South Coast Rd, Telscombe Cliffs, Peacehaven,
East Sussex BN10 7AD
Tel: 01273 584674
Real Ales, Bar Food, Restaurant Menu,
Accommodation, No Smoking Area, Disabled Facilities

185 Thatched Inn
Grand Avenue, Hassocks, Sussex BN6 8DH
Tel: 01273 842946
Real Ales, Bar Food, Restaurant Menu,
No Smoking Area, Disabled Facilities

186 Thomas-A-Beckett
146 Rectory Rd, Worthing, West Sussex BN14 7PJ
Tel: 01903 266643
Real Ales, Bar Food, Restaurant Menu,
No Smoking Area, Disabled Facilities

187 The Three Horseshoes
182 South Street, Lancing, Sussex BN15 8AU
Tel: 01903 753424
Real Ales, Bar Food, Restaurant Menu,
No Smoking Area, Disabled Facilities

188 Tiger Inn
The Green, East Dean, Eastbourne,
Sussex BN20 0DA
Tel: 01323 423209
Real Ales, Bar Food, Restaurant Menu,
Disabled Facilities

189 Toad At The Presshouse
56 Chapel Rd, Worthing, West Sussex BN11 1BE
Tel: 08703 305246
Bar Food, No Smoking Area, Disabled Facilities

190 Toby Jug Inn
Cowley Drive, Woodingdean, Brighton,
Sussex BN2 6WD
Tel: 01273 304100
Real Ales

191 Top House
Keymer Rd, Burgess Hill, West Sussex RH15 0AD
Tel: 01444 233955
Real Ales, Bar Food, No Smoking Area,
Disabled Facilities

192 Trevor Arms
The Street, Glynde, Sussex BN8 6SS
Tel: 01273 858208
Real Ales, Bar Food, No Smoking Area,
Disabled Facilities

193 **The Victoria**
1 Victoria Rd, Portslade, Brighton,
East Sussex BN41 1XP
Tel: 01273 420938
Real Ales, Bar Food, Disabled Facilities
See panel opposite

194 Vine Inn
27-29 High Street, Tarring, Worthing,
Sussex BN14 7NN
Tel: 01903 202891
Real Ales, Bar Food, No Smoking Area

195 The Vintners Parrot
10-12 Warwick Street, Worthing,
Sussex BN11 3DL
Tel: 01903 237978
Real Ales, Bar Food, Restaurant Menu,
No Smoking Area

196 Volunteer Inn
12 Eastgate Street, Lewes, East Sussex BN7 2LP
Tel: 01273 487841
Real Ales, Bar Food, No Smoking Area,
Disabled Facilities

197 The Warwick Arms
25 Warwick Street, Worthing, Sussex BN11 3DQ
Tel: 01903 206088
Real Ales, Bar Food, Restaurant Menu,
No Smoking Area, Disabled Facilities

 **The Victoria**

Victoria Road, Portslade, East Sussex BN41 1XP

☎ 01273 420938

Real Ales, Bar Food, Disabled Facilities

 In Portslade, 2 miles W of Brighton close to the A23 and A27

 Youngs, Harveys

🍴 12-7

♫ Live music Sat & Sun, karaoke Tues & Thurs

🪑 Patio

🕐 11-11 (Sun 12-10.30)

🏛 Hove 1 mile, Brighton 2 miles

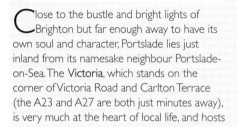

Close to the bustle and bright lights of Brighton but far enough away to have its own soul and character, Portslade lies just inland from its namesake neighbour Portslade-on-Sea. The Victoria, which stands on the corner of Victoria Road and Carlton Terrace (the A23 and A27 are both just minutes away), is very much at the heart of local life, and hosts

Clive and Annette Gauntlett extend a friendly greeting and genuine hospitality throughout the day. Youngs Bitter and Harveys Sussex Best are the resident real ales, and a selection of good honest home-cooked food is served from noon to 7 o'clock. Recently given a top-to-toe refit, the Victoria is one of Pershore's most sociable spots, with live music on Saturday and Sunday evenings and karaoke on Tuesday and Thursday.

---

198 The Weald Inn

Royal George Road, Burgess Hill, Sussex RH15 9SJ
Tel: 01444 232776

Real Ales, Bar Food, No Smoking Area,
Disabled Facilities

199 Wellington

Steyne Road, Seaford, Sussex BN25 1HT
Tel: 01323 890032

Real Ales, Bar Food, Restaurant Menu,
No Smoking Area

200 The Wheatsheaf

22-24 Richmond Rd, Worthing,
West Sussex BN11 1PP
Tel: 01903 233167

Real Ales, Bar Food, No Smoking Area

201 The Whistlestop Inn

2 Station Rd, Portslade, Brighton,
East Sussex BN41 1GA
Tel: 01273 417578

Real Ales, Bar Food

202 The White Hart

High Street, Henfield, Sussex BN5 9HP
Tel: 01273 492006

Real Ales, Bar Food, Restaurant Menu,
No Smoking Area

203 White Hart Hotel

55 High Street, Lewes, Sussex BN7 1XE
Tel: 01273 476694

Real Ales, Bar Food, Restaurant Menu,
Accommodation, No Smoking Area, Disabled Facilities

204 The White Horse Inn
23 High Street, Steyning, Sussex BN44 3YE
Tel: 01903 812347
Real Ales, Bar Food, Restaurant Menu,
No Smoking Area

205 The White Horse Inn
16 West Street, Ditchling, Hassocks,
Sussex BN6 8TS
Tel: 01273 842006
Real Ales, Bar Food, Restaurant Menu,
No Smoking Area

See panel below

206 White Horse Inn
Albourne Road, Hurstpierpoint, Hassocks,
Sussex BN6 9SP
Tel: 01273 834717
Real Ales, Bar Food, Restaurant Menu,
Accommodation, No Smoking Area

207 The Windmill Inn
180 Old Shoreham Rd, Southwick, Brighton,
East Sussex BN42 4TR
Tel: 01273 874930
Real Ales, Bar Food, Restaurant Menu,
No Smoking Area, Disabled Facilities

208 Windsor House Hotel
14-20 Windsor Road, Worthing, Sussex BN11 2LX
Tel: 01903 239655
Bar Food, Restaurant Menu, Accommodation,
No Smoking Area, Disabled Facilities

209 The Winning Post
Station Road, Plumpton Green, Lewes,
Sussex BN7 3DR
Tel: 01273 890571
Real Ales, Bar Food, Restaurant Menu

See panel opposite

---

205 The White Horse Inn

16 West Street, Ditchling, East Sussex BN16 8TS
☎ 01273 842006 (Restaurant 01273 841380)

Real Ales, Bar Food, Restaurant Menu,
No Smoking Area

- In the village of Ditchling at the junction of the B2112 and B2116
- Harveys Bitter + guest
- 12-2.30 & 6-9.30 (Sun 7-9)
- Car park, beer garden
- Major cards accepted
- All day, every day
- Ditchling Nature Reserve and Country Park 1 mile, Burgess Hill 2 miles, Plumpton racecourse 2 miles

In the heart of the village of Ditchling, the White Horse Inn is an attractive and distinctive white-painted building dating back to the 16th century. Landlords Ian and Mary Turner, along with their son Sean and daughter Emily, have been here since 1992, and their experience and knowledge of the local area continue to play a major role in the success of this former hotel. Hospitality is second to none, and the cosy bar is a perfect spot to relax over a glass of real ale. Food is an important aspect here, and the extensive menu of home-cooked dishes features both old favourites and more imaginative options on the daily specials board. There's also a separate sandwich list. Food is available every lunchtime and evening and is served on Friday and Saturday evenings and Sunday lunchtime in the 48-cover restaurant. Booking is recommended.

209 The Winning Post

Station Road, Plumpton Green, Lewes,
East Sussex BN7 3DR
☎ 01273 890571

Real Ales, Bar Food, Restaurant Menu

- ☞ Off the A275 then B2116 close to the station and racecourse
- 🍺 Harveys + guest
- ¶ 12-2.30 & 7-9 (no food Sun eve or all Mon except Bank Holidays or race days)
- ♫ Comedy evenings 1 Sunday quarterly, pool, darts
- ⛏ Car park, garden, courtyard
- 💳 Major cards except Amex and Diners
- 🕐 11-11 (Sun 12-10.30)
- 🏛 Plumpton racecourse 5 mins walk, Ditchling Country Park, Nature Reserve 2 miles, Brighton 6 miles

Followers of National Hunt racing will be aware that there are two winning posts at Plumpton Green. One is at the business end of the racecourse, the other is this friendly inn. The **Winning Post** is in the excellent care of Ken and Denise, who welcome one and all into the cosy surroundings of the bar or outside in the suntrap beer garden. A tempting range of hot and cold home-cooked dishes is served lunchtime and evening, and one Saturday a month a themed food evening is always popular.

210 Ye Old House At Home

77 Broadwater Street East, Worthing,
Sussex BN14 9AD
Tel: 01903 232661

Real Ales, Bar Food, Restaurant Menu,
No Smoking Area, Disabled Facilities

211 Ye Olde Smugglers Inne

Waterloo Square, Alfriston, Sussex BN26 5UE
Tel: 01323 870241

Real Ales, Bar Food, No Smoking Area

212 The Yew Tree Inn

Arlington, Polegate, Sussex BN26 6RX
Tel: 01323 870590

Real Ales, Restaurant Menu, No Smoking Area,
Disabled Facilities

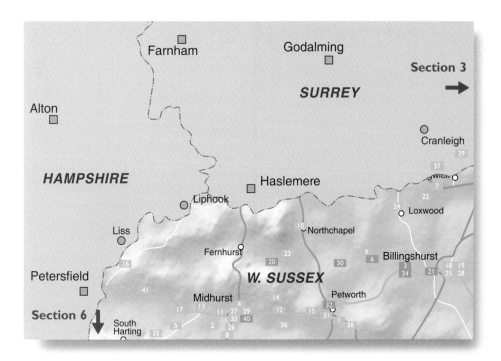

Farnham

Godalming

Section 3

SURREY

Alton

Cranleigh
39

37

HAMPSHIRE   Haslemere   wick

22

Liphook   24   Loxwood

Liss   10   Northchapel

Fernhurst   23   9   Billingshurst
16   20   30   6   3   18   19
34   21   25   28

Petersfield

W. SUSSEX   Petworth
41   Midhurst   14   32
Section 6   17   13   11   27   29   12   15   31
33   40   36   38
South   5   2   26
Harting   35   8

▦ Pub or Inn Reference Number - Detailed Information

▦ Pub or Inn Reference Number - Summary Entry

● ▦ Place of interest mentioned in the chapter introduction

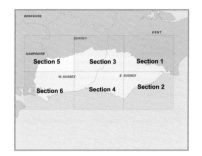

THE SUSSEX DOWNS – WEST

The South Downs is a splendid range of chalk hills that extend for over 50 miles and provide wonderful walking in an Area of Outstanding Natural Beauty. This region is home to several grand or once grand country houses, including the ruined Cowdray Park at Midhurst, Uppark and Petworth House.

Arundel

This quiet, civilised town lies beneath the battlements of one of the most imposing castles in the country. The second largest castle in England, this motte and double bailey construction has been the seat of the Dukes of Norfolk and the Earls of Arun for over 700 years.

Arundel Castle

Billingshurst

This attractive small town, strung out along the Roman Stane Street, was an important coaching town in the days before the railways, and several old coaching inns still survive. The Norman **Church of St Mary** has a clock whose mechanism is a half-size replica of Big Ben's.

Loxwood

This pleasant village near the border with Surrey stands on the **Wey and Arun Junction Canal**, which opened in 1816 and joined London with the south coast. It was closed in 1871 but certain stretches have been restored.

Midhurst

The splendid Tudor courtyard mansion of Cowdray is now in ruins, but visitors still flock here to watch the polo matches at **Cowdray Park**.

Petworth

Petworth House, built towards the end of the 17th century, looks

Petworth House

more like a French chateau than an English country mansion. It is home to the National Trust's finest collection of art from the 18th and 19th centuries, with over 300 oil paintings and 100 pieces of ancient and neo-classical sculpture. The 700-acre deer park was landscaped by Capability Brown and immortalised in paint by Turner.

South Harting

On the crest of a hill in one of the most attractive villages in the South Downs

stands late-17th century **Uppark**. The elegant interior houses an outstanding Grand Tour art collection, a famous doll's house and an exhibition explaining the history, survival and rescue of the house after a serious fire in 1989. The village church has a spire distinctively covered in copper shingles. Outside the church stand the ancient stocks and whipping post, and inside are several monuments, including one commemorating the life of Sir Harry Fetherstonhaugh of Uppark.

3 The Cricketers Arms

Wisborough Green, West Sussex RH14 0DG
☎ 01403 700369 ⊕ www.cricketersarms.com

Real Ales, Bar Food, Restaurant Menu

- ☞ Just off the A272 3 miles W of Billingshurst
- 🍺 Greene King IPA, Young's Original
- 🍴 12-2 & 6-9.30
- 🎵 Live music Thursday
- 🪑 Terrace, car park
- 🚗 Major cards accepted
- 🕐 12-11 (Sun to 10.30)
- 🏛 Billingshurst 3 miles, Petworth 6 miles

By the Green of a pretty Sussex village in undulating Weald country, the Cricketers Arms is an inn of great character. Beams at odd angles, half-panelling and period prints and pictures paint a delightfully traditional scene in the bar, where three real ales are always on tap.

Sarah Tulip was an accountant before ate about food and great care is evident in both freshness and quality of ingredients, cooking and presentation throughout the wide variety of fish, meat and vegetarian dishes.

Many of the dishes can be ordered in regular or smaller portions, including all the desserts – so no guilty feelings about giving in to the temptations of apple crumble or fudge brownies.

1 Black Horse

Byworth, Petworth, Sussex GU28 0HL
Tel: 01798 342424
Real Ales, Bar Food, Restaurant Menu

2 Country Inn

Severals Road, Bepton, Midhurst, Sussex GU29 0LR
Tel: 01730 813466
Real Ales, Bar Food, Disabled Facilities

3 The Cricketers Arms

Loxwood Road, Wisborough Green,
Sussex RH14 0DG
Tel: 01403 700369
Real Ales, Bar Food, Restaurant Menu

See panel above

4 Crown Inn

Edinburgh Square, Midhurst, Sussex GU29 9NL
Tel: 01730 813462
Real Ales

5 Elsted Inn

Elsted Marsh, Midhurst, Sussex GU29 0JT
Tel: 01730 813662
Real Ales, Bar Food, Restaurant Menu,
Accommodation, No Smoking Area, Disabled Facilities

6 The Foresters Arms

Kirdford, Billingshurst, Sussex RH14 0ND
Tel: 01403 820205
Real Ales, Bar Food, Restaurant Menu,
No Smoking Area

See panel on page 86

7 The Fox Inn

A281 Bucks Green, Rudgwick, Horsham,
Sussex RH12 3JP
Tel: 01403 822386
Real Ales, Bar Food, Restaurant Menu,
No Smoking Area, Disabled Facilities

8 Greyhound Inn

Cocking Causeway, Midhurst, Sussex GU29 9QH
Tel: 01730 814425
Real Ales, Restaurant Menu, No Smoking Area,
Disabled Facilities

6 The Foresters Arms

Kirdford, nr Billinghurst, West Sussex RH14 0ND
☎ 01403 820205

Real Ales, Bar Food, Restaurant Menu,
No Smoking Area

☛ The inn lies off the A272 between Petworth
and Billingshurst

🍺 Always 4

🍴 12-2.30 & 6-9

🎵 Regular jazz and folk nights and theme nights

⛰ Garden, car park

💳 Major cards accepted

🕐 11.30-3 & 6-11

🏛 Billingshurst 5 miles, Petworth 5 miles, Black
Down Nature Trail 8 miles

On the Green in the tiny rural village of
Kirdford, the **Foresters Arms** is a 17th
century former coaching inn with many
charming period features. The cosy interior
retains inglenook fires and stone floors, while
outside is a delightful garden with a boules
pitch, a fairy tree enchantingly lit at night and a
charming waterfall feature. Traditional home-
cooked food is served lunchtime and evening
in the non-smoking restaurant, and sandwiches,
salads and snacks cater for smaller menus;
children have their own menu, or adult meals
can also be prepared in smaller portions –
typical of the care taken by leaseholder
Marlene Oliver. Marlene and her helpers make
sure that everyone feels quickly at home in the
pub, which is not surprisingly a popular venue
for wedding receptions, promotions and other
special occasions.

9 Half Moon Inn

Petworth Road, Kirdford, Petworth,
Sussex RH14 0NU
Tel: 01403 820223
Real Ales, Bar Food, Restaurant Menu,
Accommodation, No Smoking Area

10 Half Moon Inn

Northchapel, Petworth, Sussex GU28 9HW
Tel: 01428 707270
Real Ales, Bar Food, Restaurant Menu,
Accommodation, No Smoking Area, Disabled Facilities

11 The Half Moon Inn

Petersfield Rd, Midhurst, West Sussex GU29 9LL
Tel: 01730 810818
Real Ales, Bar Food, Restaurant Menu,
No Smoking Area, Disabled Facilities

12 Halfway Bridge Inn

Lodsworth, Petworth, Sussex GU28 9BP
Tel: 01798 861281
Real Ales, Bar Food, Restaurant Menu,
No Smoking Area

13 The Hamilton Arms

School Lane, Stedham, Midhurst,
West Sussex GU29 0NZ
Tel: 01730 812555
Real Ales, Bar Food, Restaurant Menu,
No Smoking Area, Disabled Facilities

14 The Hollist Arms

The Street, Lodsworth, Petworth, Sussex GU28 9BZ
Tel: 01798 861310
Real Ales, Bar Food, Restaurant Menu,
No Smoking Area, Disabled Facilities

20 The Lickfold Inn

Lickfold, nr Midhurst, West Sussex GU28 9EY
☎ 01798 861285

Real Ales, Restaurant Menu, No Smoking Area,
Disabled Facilities

☛ On a minor road off the A272 2 miles E of
Midhurst

🍺 Horsham Best

🍴 12-2.30 & 7-9.30 (not Sun eve or Mon)

🎵 Live music last Sun of month

⛏ Garden, car park

💳 Major cards accepted

🕐 11-3.30 & 6-11 (Closed Monday)

🏛 Midhurst 2 miles, Haslemere 4 miles,
Petworth 5 miles

The Lickfold Inn is a fine Grade I listed
building dating back to 1460, located in a
picturesque little village east of Midhurst, in the
countryside above the A272 on the way to

Petworth. Behind the ornate, eyecatching brick
and timber frontage the inn is rich in traditional
appeal, with a large inglenook fireplace in the
bar and oak-beamed ceilings in the bar and
restaurant.

There are seats for 30 in the restaurant, and
for 60 more in the spacious beer garden, and
upstairs at the inn is a function room that can
seat 40. The name Lickfold is thought to derive
from a combination of Anglo-Saxon words
that can be rendered as 'the enclosure where
wild garlic grows', which explains the logo of a
head of garlic on the inn's printed menu.

The menu makes mouthwatering reading,
and results on the plate certainly live up to the
tempting descriptions. Typical dishes could
include seared scallops wrapped in Parma ham,
served on a cream and mint pea purée; terrine
of roasted Mediterranean vegetables with
baked goat's cheese on bruschetta; pan-seared
salmon on Thai potato cake with a sweet chilli
butter; and prime Scottish fillet of beef served
with a confit of vine cherry tomatoes, garlic
and thyme-roasted Portobello mushroom,
herby sautéed potatoes and a Madeira jus. The
menu changes every 4 to 6 weeks to take
advantage of the best seasonal produce, and
the blackboard menu changes daily. As well as
an award-winning destination restaurant, the
Lickfold Inn is also a country pub with a
cheerful ambience and a welcome for all the
family – and their well-behaved dogs!

The South Downs provide excellent
opportunities for taking the air and working up
a thirst and appetite, and there's plenty to
discover in the lanes and villages in the vicinity.
Lurgashall has a fine Saxon church, and just
outside Lodsworth stands St Peter's Well,
where the waters have long been thought to
have healing properties. That may or may not
be true, but there's no doubt that anyone
visiting the Lickfold Inn will leave feeling a great
deal better!

15 Horse Guards Inn
Tillington, Petworth, Sussex GU28 9AF
Tel: 01798 342332
Real Ales, Bar Food, Restaurant Menu,
Accommodation, No Smoking Area

16 Jolly Drover
Hill Brow, Liss, Sussex GU33 7QL
Tel: 01730 893137
Real Ales, Bar Food, Restaurant Menu,
No Smoking Area

17 Keepers Arms
Midhurst Road, Trotton, Sussex GU31 5ER
Tel: 01730 813724
Real Ales, Bar Food, Restaurant Menu,
No Smoking Area, Disabled Facilities

18 The Kings Arms
80 High Street, Billingshurst, Sussex RH14 9QS
Tel: 01403 782072
Real Ales

19 The Kings Head
40 High Street, Billingshurst, Sussex RH14 9NY
Tel: 01403 782921
Real Ales, Bar Food, Disabled Facilities

20 The Lickfold Inn
Lickfold, Nr Midhurst, Sussex GU28 9EY
Tel: 01798 861285
Real Ales, Restaurant Menu, No Smoking Area,
Disabled Facilities
See panel on page 87

21 The Limeburners Inn
Newbridge , Billingshurst, Sussex RH14 9JA
Tel: 01403 782311
Real Ales, Bar Food, Accommodation,
No Smoking Area
See panel adjacent

22 Mucky Duck Inn
Loxwood Road, Tismans Common, Horsham,
Sussex RH12 3BW
Tel: 01403 822300
Real Ales, Bar Food, Restaurant Menu,
Accommodation, Disabled Facilities

21 The Limeburners Inn
Lordings Road, Newbridge, Billingshurst,
West Sussex RH14 9JA
☎ 01403 782311

Real Ales, Bar Food, Accommodation,
No Smoking Area

- ☛ 100 yards off the A272 2 miles W of Billingshurst
- 🍺 HSB, Gales
- 🍴 12-2.30 & 6-9.30
- ⊢ Caravan & Camping park
- 🅿 Car park, gardens front and side
- 🚗 Major cards except Amex and Diners
- ◷ Lunchtime and evening (all day Sat & Sun in summer)
- 🏛 Wisborough Green (Church of St Peter ad Vincula) 1 mile, Billingshurst 2 miles

The focal point of a tiny village west of Billingshurst, the Limeburners Inn is an outstanding old-world hostelry. The public areas are full of period atmosphere, with beams, brasses and an open fire in a brick hearth. The inn has been in the same family for more than 50 years, and licensee Chip Sawyer is very much the life and soul of the place. He uses the best local suppliers for the home-cooked dishes served every lunchtime and evening. Behind the inn is a fully equipped caravan and camping site.

23 Noaks Ark Inn
The Green, Lurgashall, Petworth,
Sussex GU28 9ET
Tel: 01428 707346
Real Ales, Bar Food, Restaurant Menu,
No Smoking Area

24 Onslow Arms
High Street, Billingshurst, Sussex RH14 0RD
Tel: 01403 752452
Real Ales, Bar Food, Restaurant Menu,
Disabled Facilities

25 Railway Inn
40 Station Road, Billingshurst, Sussex RH14 9SE
Tel: 01403 782928
Real Ales, Bar Food, Restaurant Menu

30 The Stag

Balls Cross, Petworth, West Sussex GU28 9JP
☎ 01403 820241

Real Ales, Bar Food, Restaurant Menu,
Accommodation, No Smoking Area

- ☛ On a minor road off the A283 (Leave 1 mile N of Petworth)
- 🍺 King & Barnes, Badger Best
- 🍴 12-2 & 7-9 (not Sun eve)
- 🛏 2 rooms
- 🎵 Jazz and Blues evenings in summer
- ⛱ Beer garden, car park
- 💳 Major cards accepted
- 🏅 Midhurst Gazette's Pub of the Year 2005
- 🕐 11-3 & 6-11 (Sun 12-3 & 7-10.30)
- 🏛 Petworth House 2 miles, Billingshurst 6 miles

The Stag is a delightfully unspoilt, relaxed and convivial little pub on a former coaching route, signposted in a village off the A283 close to Petworth. Each of the rooms has its own appeal: the flagstoned bar with its winter log fire, the tiny snug next to it, the carpeted dining room with equine and country pictures, another room with Victorian prints where darts and pool are played, the two comfortable en suite bedrooms. Tenant Hamish Barrie Hiddleston and his staff have made many friends with their warm welcome and friendly, helpful service. Drinks include King & Barnes and Badger Best real ales, and wines by the glass to accompany good-value food, from filled rolls and jacket potatoes to macaroni cheese, a great fish pie, liver & bacon and seasonal game. Picnic benches at the front and in the back garden put the final touches on this inn for all seasons, a real pub-lover's pub.

26 Royal Oak
Oaklands Lane, West Lavington, Midhurst,
Sussex GU29 0EP
Tel: 01730 814611
Real Ales, Bar Food, Restaurant Menu,
Disabled Facilities

27 The Silver Horseshoe
North Street, Midhurst, Sussex GU29 9DH
Tel: 01730 817227
Real Ales, No Smoking Area

28 Six Bells
76 High Street, Billingshurst, Sussex RH14 9QS
Tel: 01403 782124
Real Ales, Bar Food, Restaurant Menu,
No Smoking Area, Disabled Facilities

29 Spreadeagle Hotel & Health Spa
South Street, Midhurst, Sussex GU29 9NH
Tel: 01730 816911
Real Ales, Bar Food, Restaurant Menu,
Accommodation, No Smoking Area

30 The Stag
Petworth Road, Balls Cross, Petworth,
Sussex GU28 9JP
Real Ales, Bar Food, Restaurant Menu,
Accommodation, No Smoking Area

See panel above

31 The Star Inn
Market Square, Petworth, West Sussex GU28 0AH
Tel: 01798 342569
Real Ales, Bar Food, Restaurant Menu

34 The Three Crowns

Wisborough Green, West Sussex RH14 0DX
☎ 01403 700207
e-mail: d-emery@btconnect.com
Proprietors: Jason & Debbie Emery

Real Ales, Bar Food, Restaurant Menu,
No Smoking Area

- ☛ On the A272 3 miles W of Billingshurst
- 🍺 Horsham Best Bitter
- 🍴 12-2 & 6-9 (Sun 12-2 & 6-9)
- ♫ Occasional jazz evenings
- ⚓ Garden, car park
- ⚡ Major cards accepted
- ⏰ 12-3 & 6-11 (Sun 12-3 & 7-10.30)
- 🏛 Billingshurst 3 miles, Petworth 6 miles

A row of adjacent buildings on the main street of Wisborough Green were combined many years ago to make the **Three Crowns**, where the promise of the immaculate outside is more than fulfilled within. Horsham Best Bitter – 'simply the best bitter' – is a popular order in the bar, which also stocks a full range of beers, lagers, wines (plenty by the glass), spirits and soft drinks. High-backed pew-style seating fills cosy corners in the rambling bar, and one of the dining areas features a changing collection of paintings for sale. The bar and non smoking restaurant menus offer a really good choice that includes classics such as burgers, beer-battered haddock, liver & bacon and steak & kidney pudding, as well as generously served composite salads and super fish specials. There is also a comprehensive A-La-Carte menu.

40 The Wheatsheaf

Wool Lane, Midhurst, West Sussex GU29 9BX
☎ 01730 813450
🌐 www.paparazzionline.co.uk

Real Ales, Bar Food, Restaurant Menu,
No Smoking Area, Disabled Facilities

- ☛ Centrally located in Midhurst
- 🍺 Sussex, Badger
- 🍴 12-2.30 & 5.30-10 (Summer all day); also open for breakfast
- ♫ Live music Sun eve
- ⚓ Courtyard
- ⚡ Major cards except Amex and Diners
- 🚫 No smoking inside
- ⏰ All day every day
- 🏛 Cowdray Park 1 mile, Lodsworth 2 miles, Petworth House 5 miles, Weald & Downland Museum 5 miles

O n a prominent corner site in the pleasant town of Midhurst, the **Wheatsheaf** is a great place to pause for drink or a meal. A recent top-to-toe refurbishment has preserved all the traditional appeal of the inn's 17th century origins, and tenant Jonathan Berry and manager Neil Sanders and their staff take excellent care of all their visitors. The food options include a full choice of vibrant contemporary cooking lunchtime and evening and all day in the summer, and sandwiches throughout the afternoon. The inn is also open for breakfast (10 to 12 Monday to Saturday, 9 to 11 on Sunday). The Sunday roast lunches are always popular, as are the barbecues that are held in the rear courtyard. A private dining room is available, located in the old chapel of this distinctive building. No smoking inside.

32 The Stonemasons Inn

North Street, Petworth, Sussex GU28 9NL
Tel: 01798 342510
Real Ales, Bar Food, Restaurant Menu,
Accommodation, No Smoking Area, Disabled Facilities

See panel adjacent

33 The Swan Inn

Red Lion Street, Midhurst, Sussex GU29 9PB
Tel: 01730 812853
Real Ales, Bar Food, No Smoking Area

34 The Three Crowns

Billingshurst Road, Wisborough Green, Billingshurst,
Sussex RH14 0DX
Tel: 01403 700207
Real Ales, Bar Food, Restaurant Menu,
No Smoking Area

See panel opposite

35 Three Horseshoes

Elsted, Midhurst, Sussex GU29 0JY
Tel: 01730 825746
Real Ales, Bar Food, Restaurant Menu,
No Smoking Area

36 Three Moles

Selham, Petworth, Sussex GU28 0PN
Tel: 01798 861303
Real Ales

37 Thurlow Arms

Baynards, Rudgwick, Horsham, Sussex RH12 3AD
Tel: 01403 822459
Real Ales

38 Welldiggers Arms

Low Heath, Petworth, Sussex GU28 0HG
Tel: 01798 342287
Real Ales, Bar Food, Restaurant Menu,
No Smoking Area

39 Wheatsheaf Inn

Ellens Green, Rudgwick, Horsham,
West Sussex RH12 3AS
Tel: 01403 822155
Real Ales, Bar Food, Restaurant Menu,
No Smoking Area

32 The Stonemasons Inn

North Street, Petworth, West Sussex GU28 9NL
☎ 01798 342510
🌐 www.thestonemasonsinn.co.uk

Real Ales, Bar Food, Restaurant Menu, Accommodation, No Smoking Area, Disabled Facilities

☛ 2 mins walk from the centre, across the road from Petworth House

🍺 London Pride, Ballards, Gales, Youngs

🍴 12-9 (Sun 12-5)

🛏 5 rooms en suite

🅿 Car park

💳 Major cards except Amex and Diners

🕐 All day every day

🏛 Petworth House and other attractions of Petworth

Petworth House is just one of many places of interest in this part of Sussex, and the **Stonemasons Inn** is an ideal base for exploring them. The core of the inn is a row of 15th century cottages, and business partners Arjen Westerdijk and Michael Huntley have put a lot of effort into preserving the best parts of its heritage. Home-cooked food is accompanied by an interesting wine list compiled by Michael, who is also a wine merchant. For guests staying awhile the inn has five en suite rooms that combine old-world character with modern amenities.

40 The Wheatsheaf

Wool Lane, Midhurst, Sussex GU29 9BX
Tel: 01730 813450
Real Ales, Bar Food, Restaurant Menu,
No Smoking Area, Disabled Facilities

See panel opposite

41 White Horse Inn

East Street, Rogate, Sussex GU31 5EA
Tel: 01730 821333
Real Ales, Bar Food, Restaurant Menu,
No Smoking Area

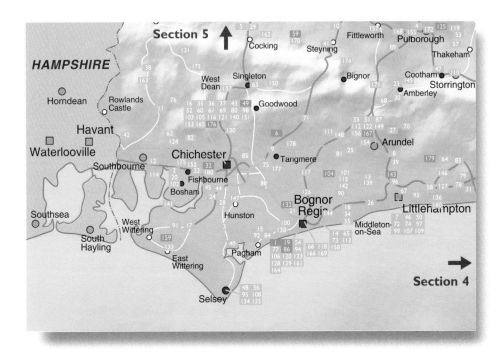

II   Pub or Inn Reference Number - Detailed Information

12   Pub or Inn Reference Number - Summary Entry

● ■ Place of interest mentioned in the chapter introduction

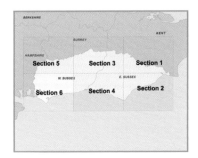

CHICHESTER AND THE WEST SUSSEX COAST

The western coastal region of West Sussex is centred round Chichester, the county town, Arundel and the resorts of Littlehampton and Bognor Regis. At Fishbourne is one of the finest Roman sites in the country, while the mosaic floors at Bignor Roman Villa near Pulborough are almost unsurpassed in Britain.

Amberley

The village church is thought to stand on the foundations of a Saxon building constructed by St Wilfrid, who converted the South Saxons to Christianity. On the site of an old chalk pit and limeworks, **Amberley Museum** concentrates on the industry of the area.

Bignor

Bignor is the site of a Roman villa, most notable for some of the finest mosaic floors in Britain. The site contains some 70 Roman buildings, and the story of the site is told in the museum.

Bognor Regis

Bognor acquired its 'Regis' suffix after a visit by King George V, who came here in 1929 to convalesce. Each year the **Birdman Rally**, in which competitors hurl themselves off the pier in an attempt to make the longest man-powered flight, attracts huge crowds.

Bosham

Known as the place where King Canute ordered back the waves, Bosham is now a favourite yachting centre. The **Bosham**

Bosham

Walk Craft Centre is a fascinating collection of little shops specialising in arts, crafts, antiques and fashion.

Chichester

In the heart of a city used by Roman legions as a base camp, **Chichester Cathedral** has been a centre for Christian worship for over 900 years. It is filled with treasures ancient and modern, including Norman sculptures, the shrine of St Richard, an altar tapestry by John Piper, a stained-glass window by Marc Chagall and a painting by Graham Sutherland of Christ appearing to Mary Magdalene.

Weald and Downland Open Air Museum, Singleton

Cootham

The village is synonymous with **Parham**, a very grand Elizabethan mansion with magnificent rooms and important collections of period furniture, Oriental carpets, rare needlework and fine paintings.

Fishbourne

Known far and wide for the splendid Roman remains discovered in 1960. **Fishbourne Roman Palace** was built around AD75 for the Celtic king Cogibundus as a reward for collaborating with the Roman conquerors.

Goodwood

Goodwood House is the spectacular country home of the Dukes of Richmond. The original modest hunting lodge still stands in the grounds but has been superseded by the present 18th century mansion, built on a grand scale by the architect James Wyatt. The 12,000-acre estate on which the house stands incorporates Goodwood racecourse.

Selsey

Among the striking buildings here is **Selsey Windmill**, a redbrick tower mill dating from 1820.

Singleton

Here is located the renowned **Weald and Downland Open Air Museum**, which comprises over 40 reconstructed buildings brought from all over southeast England.

Tangmere

Tangmere is very much associated with its Battle of Britain Base, and the heroic deeds of the pilots are remembered in the local pub (The Bader Arms) and the **Tangmere Military Aviation Museum**.

1 The Alex

56 London Road, Bognor Regis, Sussex PO21 1PU
Tel: 01243 863308

Real Ales, Bar Food, Restaurant Menu,
No Smoking Area

See panel below

2 The Anchor Bleu

High Street, Chichester, Sussex PO18 8LS
Tel: 01243 573956

Real Ales, Bar Food, Restaurant Menu,
No Smoking Area

1 The Alex

56 London Road, Bognor Regis,
East Sussex PO21 1PU
☎ 01243 863308

Real Ales, Bar Food, Restaurant Menu,
No Smoking Area

 Centrally located in Bognor Regis

 Courage Best, Greene King Abbot

🍴 10-2 (Sun 12-1.45)

🚫 No children

🕐 10am-11pm (Sun 12-5)

🏛 All the attractions of Bognor; Arundel 6 miles

Good hospitality, good beer and good food are assured by Martyn and Janet Borrill, the friendly, outgoing tenants of **The Alex**. Formerly called the Alexandra Tavern and dating from the 1860s, the inn enjoys a central location in Bognor Regis. Shoppers, workers, local residents and visitors to the 'Sunshine Capital' of Britain all find it an excellent place for taking a break. Three real ales – Courage Best, Greene King Abbot and a Guest Ale – are always available, and home-cooked dishes are served from opening time to 2 o'clock. An eye-catching feature in the bar is a collection of more than 1,000 mugs.

3 The Anchor Inn

Selsey Road, Sidlesham, Chichester,
Sussex PO20 7QU
Tel: 01243 641373

Real Ales, Bar Food, Restaurant Menu,
Accommodation, No Smoking Area, Disabled Facilities

4 The Anchor Inn

46 High Street, Pulborough, Sussex RH20 4DU
Tel: 01903 742665

Real Ales, Bar Food, Restaurant Menu,
No Smoking Area, Disabled Facilities

5 Angel Hotel

North Street, Midhurst, Sussex GU29 9DN
Tel: 01730 812421

Bar Food, Accommodation, No Smoking Area,
Disabled Facilities

6 The Anglesey Arms

Stane St., Halnaker, Chichester, Sussex PO18 0NQ
Tel: 01243 773474

Real Ales, Bar Food, Restaurant Menu,
No Smoking Area

See panel on page 96

7 Arun View Inn

Old Customs House Wharf Road, Littlehampton,
Sussex BN17 5DD
Tel: 01903 722335

Real Ales, Bar Food, Restaurant Menu,
Accommodation, No Smoking Area, Disabled Facilities

8 Arundel Park Hotel

Station Road, Arundel, Sussex BN18 9PH
Tel: 01903 882588

Real Ales, Bar Food, Restaurant Menu,
Accommodation, No Smoking Area

9 Bader Arms

Malcolm Road, Tangmer, Chichester,
Sussex PO20 2HS
Tel: 01243 779422

Real Ales, Bar Food, Restaurant Menu,
Disabled Facilities

The Anglesey Arms

Stane Street, Halnaker, nr Chichester,
West Sussex PO18 0NQ

☎ 01243 773474 ⊕ www.angleseyarms.co.uk

Real Ales, Bar Food, Restaurant Menu,
No Smoking Area

- On the A285 Chichester-Petworth road 3 miles NE of Chichester
- Youngs, Adnams, Caledonian
- 12-2.30 & 6.30-9.30
- Theme food nights
- Garden, meadow, orchard, car park
- Major cards except Amex & Diners
- 11-3 & 5.30-11 (all day Sat & Sun)
- Goodwood 2 miles, Fontwell Park 2 miles, Chichester 3 miles

Behind a very handsome redbrick frontage, the **Anglesey Arms** is one of the most delightful pubs in the region, with a total lack of pretension and a warm, inviting ambience generated by hosts Roger and Jools Jackson and their staff. Furnished with sturdy country chairs and tables, the bar is a great spot for enjoying a drink and a lively chat, and lovers of real ales will fine plenty of choice. The high standard of cooking is another plus here, and the lunchtime menu proposes made–to-order sandwiches, ploughman's platters, omelettes, pasta and classics such as home-baked ham, fish cakes and beer-battered cod. Steaks are a speciality both at lunchtime and in the evening, when other main courses feature pork and lamb from the Goodwood Estate, on which the pub stands. Children are welcome in the non-smoking dining room and in the 2-acre grounds, which include gardens, an orchard and a meadow.

---

10 Badgers Tavern

Coultershaw Bridge, Petworth,
Sussex GU28 0JF
Tel: 01798 342651

Real Ales, Bar Food, Restaurant Menu,
Accommodation, No Smoking Area

11 The Barley Mow

Walderton, Chichester, Sussex PO18 9ED
Tel: 02392 631321

Real Ales, Bar Food, Restaurant Menu,
No Smoking Area, Disabled Facilities

12 The Barleycorn

Main Road, Nutbourne, Chichester,
Sussex PO18 8RS
Tel: 01243 573172

Real Ales, Bar Food, Restaurant Menu,
No Smoking Area, Disabled Facilities

13 Barnham Bridge Inn

28 Barnham Road, Barnham, Sussex BN18 0BJ
Tel: 01243 552272

Real Ales, Bar Food, Restaurant Menu,
No Smoking Area, Disabled Facilities

14 Beachcroft

Clyde Road, Bognor Regis, Sussex PO22 7AH
Tel: 01243 827142

Bar Food, Restaurant Menu, Accommodation

15 The Bear Inn

237 Pagham Road, Pagham, Bognor Regis,
Sussex PO21 3QB
Tel: 01243 262157

Real Ales, Bar Food, Restaurant Menu,
Accommodation, No Smoking Area, Disabled Facilities

19 The Berkeley Arms

25/27 West Street, Bognor Regis,
West Sussex PO21 1XA
☎ 01243 826878

Real Ales, Bar Food, Restaurant Menu, Accommodation, No Smoking Area, Disabled Facilities

 150 yards from the seafront in Bognor
 London Pride + guests
 12-8
 6 rooms
 Pool and darts teams, golf society
 Major cards accepted
⏲ All day every day
🏛 Seafront short walk; Arundel 6 miles, Chichester 6 miles

A short stroll from the seafront in Bognor Regis, the Berkeley Arms is easy to spot with its gabled facade and small-paned windows. The inside is equally distinctive, with red-painted beams and ceilings, and country furniture and pew-style benches adding to the inviting, traditional feel. But the building actually only dates from 1933, when the Wheatsheaf Hotel was demolished and the Berkeley Arms took its place, moving lock, stock and barrel from No 33 in the same street.

London Pride is the resident cask ale, and good-value food ranges from sandwiches and basket meals to fish & chips with mushy peas, chicken hotpot and the day's roasts with all the trimmings. The inn plays an important part in Bognor's social life, with darts and pool teams, a golf society and regular charity activities supporting good causes such as local hospices.

---

16 The Bell Inn

3 Broyle Road, Chichester, Sussex PO19 7AT
Tel: 01243 783388

Real Ales, Bar Food, Restaurant Menu,
No Smoking Area, Disabled Facilities

17 The Bell Inn

Bell Lane, Birdham, Chichester, Sussex PO20 7HY
Tel: 01243 514338

Real Ales, Bar Food, Restaurant Menu,
Accommodation, No Smoking Area

18 Beresford

Elmer Road, Middleton-On-Sea, Bognor Regis,
Sussex PO22 6EH
Tel: 01243 582049

Real Ales, Bar Food, Restaurant Menu,
No Smoking Area, Disabled Facilities

19 The Berkeley Arms

25/27 West Street, Bognor Regis,
Sussex PO21 1XA
Tel: 01243 826878

Real Ales, Bar Food, Restaurant Menu,
Accommodation, No Smoking Area, Disabled Facilities

See panel above

20 The Berkeley Arms

Bosham Lane, Bosham, Chichester,
Sussex PO18 8HG
Tel: 01243 573167

Real Ales, Bar Food, Restaurant Menu,
No Smoking Area

21 Bersted Tavern

351 Chichester Road, North Bersted, Bognor Regis,
Sussex PO21 5AN
Tel: 01243 823744

Real Ales, Bar Food, Restaurant Menu,
No Smoking Area, Disabled Facilities

22 The Black Boy Inn

Main Rd, Fishbourne, Chichester,
West Sussex PO18 8XX
Tel: 01243 575478

Real Ales, Bar Food, Restaurant Menu,
Accommodation, No Smoking Area, Disabled Facilities

23 Black Horse

High Street, Amberley, Arundel, Sussex BN18 9NL
Tel: 01798 831552

Real Ales, Bar Food, Restaurant Menu,
No Smoking Area

24 Black Horse

Birdham Road, Chichester, Sussex PO20 7EH
Tel: 01243 784068

Real Ales, Bar Food, Restaurant Menu,
No Smoking Area, Disabled Facilities

25 The Black Horse

Binsted, Arundel, Sussex BN18 0LP
Tel: 01243 551213

Real Ales, Bar Food, Restaurant Menu,
No Smoking Area, Disabled Facilities

26 The Black Horse

Climping Street, Climping, Littlehampton,
Sussex BN17 5RL
Tel: 01903 715175

Real Ales, Bar Food, Restaurant Menu,
No Smoking Area, Disabled Facilities

27 Black Rabbit

Mill Road, Offham, Arundel, Sussex BN18 9PB
Tel: 01903 882828

Real Ales, Bar Food, Restaurant Menu,
No Smoking Area, Disabled Facilities

28 Blacksmiths Arms

Blacksmiths Cottages, Selsey Road, Donnington,
Sussex PO20 7PR
Tel: 01243 783999

Real Ales, Bar Food, Restaurant Menu,
No Smoking Area

29 The Bricklayers Arms

Wool Lane, Midhurst, Sussex GU29 9BX
Tel: 01730 812084

Real Ales, Bar Food, Restaurant Menu,
No Smoking Area

32 The Bulls Head

Fishbourne, Chichester, West Sussex PO19 3JP
☎ 01243 839895

Real Ales, Bar Food, Restaurant Menu,
Accommodation, No Smoking Area

☛ Close to the centre of Fishbourne, 2 miles W of Chichester

🍺 Fullers London Pride, HSB, Gales Best, Butser

🍴 Lunch & Dinner

🛏 1 twin room en suite

🎵 Jazz nights

⚓ Beer garden, car park

💳 Major cards accepted

🕐 11-3 & 6-11 (all day Sat & Sun)

🏛 Bosham 2 miles, Chichester 2 miles

Starting life in the 17th century as a farmhouse, the **Bulls Head** is an attractive black-and-white listed building in the centre of Fishbourne. Under experienced licensee's Julie and Roger, the inn has gained a fine reputation for a high standard of hospitality that attracts both locals and visitors. A warm, welcoming place, it offers a good range of real ales on tap and a super menu of generously served, value-for-money dishes. The specials board proposes a long list typified by chicken breast with a bacon and stilton sauce, home-made steak & ale pie, Italian-style meatballs with pasta, salmon hollandaise and butternut squash bake. A large family room is available on a Bed & Breakfast basis. The Bulls Head is justly famous for its jazz nights, which have attracted such luminaries of jazz as Ronnie Scott.

30 The Bridge Inn
Houghton, Arundel, Sussex BN18 9LR
Tel: 01798 831619
Real Ales, Bar Food, No Smoking Area

31 The Bull Inn
Goring Street, Goring-By-Sea, Worthing,
Sussex BN12 5AR
Tel: 01903 248133
Real Ales, Restaurant Menu, No Smoking Area

32 The Bulls Head
Fishbourne Road, Fishbourne, Chichester,
Sussex PO19 3JP
Tel: 01243 839895
Real Ales, Bar Food, Restaurant Menu,
Accommodation, No Smoking Area

See panel opposite

33 Butlers Bar & Restaurant
25 Tarrant Street, Arundel, Sussex BN18 9DG
Tel: 01903 882222
Bar Food, Restaurant Menu, No Smoking Area

34 The Cabin
167-169 Elmer Road, Elmer Sands, Bognor Regis,
Sussex PO22 6JA
Tel: 01243 585643
Real Ales, Bar Food

35 The Chequers Inn
203 Oving Road, Chichester,
West Sussex PO19 7ER
Tel: 01243 786427
Real Ales, Bar Food, No Smoking Area

36 The Chichester
38 West Street, Chichester, Sussex PO19 1RP
Tel: 01243 783185
Real Ales, Bar Food, Restaurant Menu,
Accommodation, No Smoking Area

37 Coach & Horses
125B St Pancras Avenue, Chichester,
Sussex PO19 7LH
Tel: 01243 782313
Real Ales

38 Coach & Horses
The Square, Compton, Sussex PO18 9HA
Tel: 02392 631228
Real Ales, Bar Food, Restaurant Menu,
No Smoking Area

39 Comfort Inn
Lyminster Road, Littlehampton, Sussex BN17 7QQ
Tel: 01903 840840
Bar Food, Restaurant Menu, Accommodation,
No Smoking Area, Disabled Facilities

40 Crab & Lobster Public House
Mill Lane, Sidlesham, Chichester, Sussex PO20 7NB
Tel: 01243 641233
Real Ales, Bar Food, No Smoking Area,
Disabled Facilities

41 Cricketers
Duncton, Petworth, Sussex GU28 0LB
Tel: 01798 342473
Real Ales, Bar Food, Restaurant Menu,
No Smoking Area

42 Cricketers Inn
Commonside, Westbourne, Sussex PO10 8TA
Tel: 01243 372647
Real Ales

43 Crispins
46 East Street, Chichester, Sussex PO19 1HX
Tel: 01243 533544
Real Ales, Bar Food, Restaurant Menu

44 Crouchers Bottom Country Hotel
Birdham Road, Apuldram, Chichester,
Sussex PO20 7EH
Tel: 01243 784995
Real Ales, Restaurant Menu, Accommodation,
No Smoking Area, Disabled Facilities

45 Crown & Anchor
Dell Quay Road, Chichester, Sussex PO20 7EE
Tel: 01243 781712
Real Ales, Restaurant Menu, No Smoking Area

49 The Crown Inn

140 Whyke Road, Chichester,
West Sussex PO19 8HT
☎ 01243 785009

Real Ales, Bar Food, Restaurant Menu,
No Smoking Area, Disabled Facilities

 200 yards from the A27/B2145 roundabout
 Greene King IPA, Abbot
 Lunch & Dinner
 2 rooms en suite
 Jazz Friday evening
 Car park
 Major cards accepted
 12-11 (Fri, Sat from 11, Sun 12-10.30)
🏛 All the attractions of Chichester; Goodwood
2 miles

A row of white-painted fencing, a brick buttress and a roof tiling that curves round the little top-floor windows are distinctive features of the Crown Inn, which stands close to the A27/B2145 roundabout east of Chichester. The inside of the pub is no less eyecatching, with beams and exposed brick, and at the back is a delightful garden with picnic benches under parasols, trees, statues and a play area guaranteed to keep the little ones happy – and all within a stone's throw of the city centre. The Crown is very much food-oriented, and the printed menu and daily specials provide plenty of choice for all tastes and appetites. Regular jazz nights are a popular feature, and the pub's two guest bedrooms provide a comfortable and convenient base for both business and leisure travellers.

---

46 The Crown Hotel
29 High Street, Littlehampton, Sussex BN17 5EG
Tel: 01903 731784
Real Ales, Bar Food, Restaurant Menu,
No Smoking Area, Disabled Facilities

47 Crown Inn
Pulborough Road, Cootham, Pulborough,
Sussex RH20 4JN
Tel: 01903 742625
Real Ales, Bar Food, Restaurant Menu,
No Smoking Area

48 The Crown Inn
107 High Street, Chichester, Sussex PO20 0QL
Tel: 01243 602123
Real Ales, Disabled Facilities

49 The Crown Inn
140 Whyke Road, Chichester, Sussex PO19 8HT
Tel: 01243 785009
Real Ales, Bar Food, Restaurant Menu,
No Smoking Area, Disabled Facilities
See panel above

50 The Dolphin Hotel
34 High Street, Littlehampton, Sussex BN17 5ED
Tel: 01903 715789
Real Ales, Bar Food, Restaurant Menu,
No Smoking Area, Disabled Facilities

51 The Eagle Inn
41 Tarrant Street, Arundel, Sussex BN18 9DJ
Tel: 01903 882304
Real Ales

59 The Foresters Arms

Graffham, Petworth, West Sussex GU28 0QA
☎ 01798 867202

Real Ales, Bar Food, Restaurant Menu

- 🖝 3 miles S of Midhurst off the A272 or A286
- 🍺 3 rotating, mainly local
- 🍴 L & D (not Sun eve in winter or all Mon autumn and winter)
- 🛏 2 rooms en suite
- 🚗 Car park
- 💳 Major cards except Amex and Diners
- 🕐 Lunchtime and evening (all day Sat & Sun in summer)
- 🏛 Midhurst 3 miles, Petworth 5 miles

The rolling chalk hills of the South Downs are a magnet for walkers and lovers of wide open spaces, and the **Foresters Arms** is an ideal place to pause for a drink, to settle down to a snack or a meal or to stay for a night or longer. The inn dates back to the 16th century, and the old beams and the open fire provide a warm, welcoming ambience in which to enjoy a glass or two of real ale in the bar. Leaseholders Serena and Nick extend the friendliest of welcomes to one and all, and Nick, a professional chef, produces an across-the-board menu to please all tastes: typical dishes might include lentil & ham soup, game terrine, the day's fish special (always in demand) and a very tasty beef & ale pie. The guest accommodation comprises two en suite rooms next to the main building; the tariff includes breakfast in the form of a luxury hamper.

---

52 The Eastgate Inn
4 The Hornet, Chichester, Sussex PO19 7JG
Tel: 01243 774877
Real Ales, Bar Food, No Smoking Area

53 Elephant & Castle
Church Street, West Chiltington, Pulborough, Sussex RH20 2JW
Tel: 01798 813307
Real Ales, Bar Food, Restaurant Menu

54 Elizabeth II
3 The Steyne, Bognor Regis, Sussex PO21 1TX
Tel: 01243 865751
Real Ales

55 Elmer Inn
89 Elmer Road, Middleton-On-Sea, Bognor Regis, Sussex PO22 6HD
Tel: 01243 855580
Real Ales, Bar Food, Restaurant Menu, Accommodation, No Smoking Area, Disabled Facilities

56 The Fishermans Joy
71 East Street, Selsey, Chichester, Sussex PO20 0BU
Tel: 01243 602121
Real Ales, Bar Food, Restaurant Menu, No Smoking Area, Disabled Facilities

57 Five Bells
Smock Alley, West Chiltington, Sussex RH20 2QX
Tel: 01798 812143
Real Ales, Bar Food, Restaurant Menu, Accommodation

58 Fletcher Arms
Station Road, Littlehampton, Sussex BN16 3AF
Tel: 01903 784858
Real Ales, Bar Food, Restaurant Menu, Disabled Facilities

59 The Foresters Arms
Graffham, Petworth, Sussex GU28 0QA
Tel: 01798 867202
Real Ales, Bar Food, Restaurant Menu
See panel above

60 The Fountain

29 Southgate, Chichester, Sussex PO19 1ES
Tel: 01243 781352

Real Ales, Bar Food, Restaurant Menu,
No Smoking Area, Disabled Facilities

61 Four Chestnuts

Oving Road, Chichester, Sussex PO19 7EQ
Tel: 01243 779974

Real Ales, Bar Food, Restaurant Menu,
No Smoking Area

62 Fox & Hounds

Funtington, Chichester, Sussex PO18 9LL
Tel: 01243 575246

Real Ales, Bar Food, Restaurant Menu,
No Smoking Area

63 Fox Goes Free

Charlton, Chichester, Sussex PO18 0HU
Tel: 01243 811461

Real Ales, Bar Food, Restaurant Menu,
Accommodation, No Smoking Area

64 Fox Inn

Arundel Road, Patching, Worthing,
Sussex BN13 3UJ
Tel: 01903 871299

Real Ales, Restaurant Menu, No Smoking Area

65 The Fox Inn

Waterloo Road, Bognor Regis, Sussex PO22 7EH
Tel: 01243 865308

Real Ales, Bar Food

66 The Friary Arms

Shripney Road, Bognor Regis, Sussex PO22 9LN
Tel: 01243 823373

Real Ales, Disabled Facilities

67 The General Henrys

31 Horsham Road, Littlehampton,
Sussex BN17 6BZ
Tel: 01903 716570

Real Ales, Disabled Facilities

68 George & Dragon

Houghton, Amberley, Arundel, Sussex BN18 9LW
Tel: 01798 831559

Real Ales, Bar Food, Restaurant Menu,
No Smoking Area

69 George & Dragon

51 North Street, Chichester, Sussex PO19 1NQ
Tel: 01243 785660

Real Ales, Bar Food, Restaurant Menu,
Accommodation, No Smoking Area

70 George & Dragon Inn

Burpham, Arundel, Sussex BN18 9RR
Tel: 01903 883131

Real Ales, Bar Food, Restaurant Menu,
No Smoking Area, Disabled Facilities

71 George Inn

Brittens Lane, Eartham, Chichester, Sussex PO18 0LT
Tel: 01243 814340

Real Ales, Bar Food, Restaurant Menu,
Accommodation, No Smoking Area, Disabled Facilities

72 George Inn

14 Surrey St, Littlehampton, West Sussex BN17 5BG
Tel: 01903 739863

Real Ales, Bar Food, Restaurant Menu,
No Smoking Area, Disabled Facilities

73 The George Inn

102 Felpham Rd, Bognor Regis,
West Sussex PO22 7PL
Tel: 01243 824177

Real Ales, Bar Food, Restaurant Menu,
No Smoking Area

74 Globe Inn

Duke St, Littlehampton, West Sussex BN17 6EU
Tel: 01903 716557

Real Ales, Restaurant Menu, No Smoking Area

75 Gribble Inn Brewery

Gribble Lane, Oving, Sussex PO20 2BP
Tel: 01243 786893

Real Ales, Bar Food, Restaurant Menu,
No Smoking Area, Disabled Facilities

76 Hare & Hounds
Stoughton, Chichester, Sussex PO18 9JQ
Tel: 02392 631433
Real Ales, Bar Food, Restaurant Menu,
No Smoking Area

77 Hatters Inn
2-10 Queensway, Bognor Regis, Sussex PO21 1QT
Tel: 01243 840206
Real Ales, Bar Food, Restaurant Menu,
No Smoking Area, Disabled Facilities

78 The Henty Arms
2 Ferring Lane, Ferring, Worthing, Sussex BN12 6QY
Tel: 01903 241254
Real Ales, Bar Food, Restaurant Menu,
No Smoking Area, Disabled Facilities

79 Highdown Towers Hotel
Littlehampton Road, Goring By Sea, Worthing,
Sussex BN12 6PF
Tel: 01903 700152
Real Ales, Restaurant Menu, Accommodation,
No Smoking Area, Disabled Facilities

80 Hole In The Wall
1 St. Martins St, Chichester,
West Sussex PO19 1NP
Tel: 01243 533182
Real Ales, Bar Food, Restaurant Menu,
No Smoking Area

81 Hollytree Public House
The Street, Walberton, Arundel,
Sussex BN18 0PH
Tel: 01243 554023
Real Ales, Bar Food, Restaurant Menu,
Accommodation

82 Horse & Groom
East Ashling, Chichester, Sussex PO18 9AX
Tel: 01243 575339
Real Ales, Bar Food, Restaurant Menu,
Accommodation, No Smoking Area, Disabled Facilities

83 The Horse & Groom
Arundel Road, Patching, Worthing,
Sussex BN13 3UQ
Tel: 01903 871346
Real Ales, Bar Food, Restaurant Menu,
No Smoking Area, Disabled Facilities

84 The Inglenook Hotel
255 Pagham Road, Nyetimber, Sussex PO213QB
Tel: 01243 262495
Real Ales, Bar Food, Restaurant Menu,
Accommodation, No Smoking Area, Disabled Facilities

85 Jarvis Chichester Hotel
Madgwick Lane, Westhampnett, Chichester,
Sussex PO19 7QL
Tel: 01243 786351
Bar Food, Restaurant Menu, Accommodation,
No Smoking Area, Disabled Facilities

86 The Junction
13 High St, Bognor Regis, West Sussex PO21 1RJ
Tel: 01243 865789
Real Ales
See panel on page 104

87 Kings Arms
36 Tarrant Street, Arundel, Sussex BN18 9DN
Tel: 01903 882312
Real Ales, Disabled Facilities

88 The Kings Head
Bognor Road, Merston, Chichester, Sussex PO20 2EH
Tel: 01243 783576
Real Ales, Bar Food, Restaurant Menu,
Disabled Facilities

89 The Labouring Man
Old London Road, Cold Waltham, Pulborough,
Sussex RH20 1LF
Tel: 01798 872215
Real Ales, Bar Food, Restaurant Menu,
Accommodation, No Smoking Area, Disabled Facilities

86 The Junction

High Street, Bognor Regis, West Sussex PO21 1RJ
☎ 01243 865789

Real Ales, Bar Food

🏴 In the centre of Bognor

🍺 Fullers London Pride, Greene King Abbot

🍴 12-3 Mon-Sun

🎵 Live music Fri & Sat, Sky Sports Wed,Sat & Sun

💳 Major cards accepted

🕐 10.30am-11pm Mon-Wed, 10.30am-Midnight Thurs, 10.30am-01.00 Fri & Sat, Noon-Midnight Sun (as of end November 05)

🏛 Fontwell Park 5 miles, Arundel 6 miles, Chichester 6 miles

There are many very good reasons for visiting Bognor Regis, which holds the title of the sunshine capital of Britain. King George V really put the place on the map when he visited in 1929 and bestowed the royal suffix (Regis means 'of the King'). The fine buildings, the gardens, the museums and the annual Birdman Rally are among the other attractions, but for anyone wanting to enjoy a combination of a buzzy atmosphere, a good choice of drinks and regular live music sessions, the Junction is definitely the place to head for. In a prime position among the shops on Bognor's High Street, landlord Chris Lloyd keeps an impressive selection of ales, lagers and shots, to enjoy on their own or to accompany the straightforward pub dishes that are available all day. Live music sessions take place Thursday to Sunday evenings, pool and darts are played in the bar, and a huge plasma screen shows the big sporting events. The Junction is very much a place for the young at heart, but not for children.

90 Lamb Inn

Bilsham Road, Yapton, Arundel, Sussex BN18 0JN
Tel: 01243 551232

Real Ales, Bar Food, Restaurant Menu,
No Smoking Area, Disabled Facilities

91 Lamb Inn

Chichester Road, West Wittering, Chichester,
Sussex PO20 8QA
Tel: 01243 511105

Real Ales, Bar Food, Restaurant Menu,
No Smoking Area

92 The Lamb Inn

144 Pagham Road, Bognor Regis, Sussex PO21 4NJ
Tel: 01243 262168

Real Ales, Bar Food, Restaurant Menu,
No Smoking Area, Disabled Facilities

93 The Lamb Inn

73 The Street, Littlehampton, Sussex BN16 3NU
Tel: 01903 783227

Real Ales, Bar Food, Restaurant Menu,
No Smoking Area, Disabled Facilities

94 The Lamb Inn

Steyne Street, Bognor Regis, Sussex PO21 1TJ
Tel: 01243 868215

Real Ales, Bar Food, Disabled Facilities

95 The Lifeboat Inn

26 Albion Rd, Selsey, Chichester,
West Sussex PO20 0DJ
Tel: 01243 603501

Real Ales, Bar Food, Restaurant Menu,
No Smoking Area, Disabled Facilities

104 The Murrell Arms

Yapton Road, Barnham, West Sussex PO22 0AS

☎ 01243 553320

Real Ales, Bar Food, Accommodation, Disabled Facilities

➤ From the A27 at Fontwell take the A29 then the B2233 to Barnham.

🍺 Gales HSB, BBB

🍴 Lunchtime & Evening

🎵 Traditional pub games

⚓ Gardens, off-road parking

🚫 Well behaved children and dogs only

🕐 11-2.30 & 6-11

🏛 Denmans Garden 2 miles, Fontwell racecourse 3 miles, Bognor 4 miles, Chichester 5 miles

Pubs don't come much more delightful and inviting than the Murrell Arms, built as a farmhouse in 1750 and licensed since 1866. Its greatest asset is its landlord Mervyn Cotton, who has been at the helm for more than 40 years, and the large band of loyal regulars is proof that Mervyn and his wife know exactly what their customers want. Window boxes and flower tubs make a colourful show outside, while in the bars and dining areas there's a merry jumble of old posters, paintings, period photographs, horse tackle, brasses, jugs and bottles. The gardens are no less appealing, with plenty of seats and interesting features such as a well and a cider press. George Gale & Co Ltd are the owning brewery, and their excellent ales head the list of drinks. Bar snacks and meals put the emphasis on good honest flavours in dishes like macaroni cheese casserole (an all too rare treat!) and the bacon hock that's long been a great favourite with the locals.

96 The Locomotive

74 Lyminster Road, Wick, Littlehampton, Sussex BN17 7LW
Tel: 01903 716658

Real Ales, Bar Food, Restaurant Menu, No Smoking Area, Disabled Facilities

97 The Locomotive Inn

5 Terminus Road, Littlehampton, Sussex BN17 5BS
Tel: 01903 716028

Real Ales, Bar Food

98 Mainline Tavern

35 Whyke Road, Chichester, Sussex PO19 8HW
Tel: 01243 782238

Real Ales, Bar Food, Restaurant Menu, No Smoking Area

99 Marine Hotel

Selborne Road, Littlehampton, Sussex BN17 5NN
Tel: 01903 721476

Real Ales

100 The Martlets

Aldwick Road, Bognor Regis, Sussex PO21 3AD
Tel: 01243 863560

Restaurant Menu, Accommodation, No Smoking Area, Disabled Facilities

101 Maypole Inn

Maypole Lane, Yapton, Arundel, Sussex BN18 0DP
Tel: 01243 551417

Real Ales, Bar Food, Restaurant Menu, No Smoking Area, Disabled Facilities

102 Millstream Hotel & Restaurant

Bosham Lane, Bosham, Chichester,
Sussex PO18 8HL
Tel: 01243 573234

Bar Food, Restaurant Menu, Accommodation,
No Smoking Area, Disabled Facilities

103 The Mitre

Oliver Whitby Road, Chichester, Sussex PO19 3LB
Tel: 01243 785942

Real Ales

104 The Murrell Arms

Yapton Road, Barnham, Bognor Regis,
Sussex PO22 0AS
Tel: 01243 553320

Real Ales, Bar Food, Disabled Facilities

See panel on page 105

105 The Nags Head

3 St Pancras, Chichester, Sussex PO19 1SL
Tel: 01243 785823

Real Ales, Bar Food, Restaurant Menu,
Accommodation, No Smoking Area, Disabled Facilities

106 Navigator Hotel

Marine Drive West, Aldwick, Bognor Regis,
Sussex PO21 2QA
Tel: 01243 864844

Real Ales, Bar Food, Restaurant Menu,
Accommodation, No Smoking Area

107 The Nelson

61 Pier Road, Littlehampton, Sussex BN17 5LP
Tel: 01903 713358

Real Ales, Bar Food, Accommodation,
Disabled Facilities

108 Neptune Inn

120 High Street, Selsey, Sussex PO20 0QE
Tel: 01243 601022

Real Ales, Bar Food

109 The New Inn

5 Norfolk Road, Littlehampton, Sussex BN17 5PL
Tel: 01903 713112

Real Ales, Bar Food, Accommodation

110 New Moon

13 High Street, Storrington, Pulborough,
Sussex RH20 4DR
Tel: 01903 744773

Real Ales, Bar Food, Restaurant Menu,
No Smoking Area

111 Newburgh Arms

School Hill, Slindon, Arundel, Sussex BN18 0RS
Tel: 01243 814229

Real Ales, Bar Food, No Smoking Area

112 Norfolk Arms Hotel & Restaurant

High Street, Arundel, Sussex BN18 9AD
Tel: 01903 882101

Real Ales, Bar Food, Restaurant Menu,
Accommodation, No Smoking Area

113 Old Barn Free House

42 Felpham Road, Felpham, Bognor Regis,
Sussex PO22 7DF
Tel: 01243 821564

Real Ales, No Smoking Area, Disabled Facilities

114 Old House At Home

Cot Lane, Chidham, Chichester, Sussex PO18 8SU
Tel: 01243 572477

Real Ales, Bar Food, Restaurant Menu,
No Smoking Area, Disabled Facilities

115 The Olive Branch

North End Road, Yapton, Arundel,
Sussex BN18 0DU
Tel: 01243 551310

Real Ales, Bar Food, Restaurant Menu,
No Smoking Area, Disabled Facilities

125 **The Rising Sun**

The Street, Nutbourne, nr Pulborough,
West Sussex RH20 2HE
☎ 01798 812191

Real Ales, Bar Food, Restaurant Menu,
No Smoking Area

☞ On a country road off the A283 2 miles E of Pulborough

🍺 Five changes ales

🍴 12-2 & 7-9.30

🎵 Regular live entertainment

🛆 Garden

💳 Major cards accepted

🕐 11-3 & 6-11

🏛 Pulborough 2 miles, South Downs Way 4 miles, Billingshurst 6 miles

In a village setting off the A283 east of Pulborough, the 16th century Rising Sun is a splendid free house with a flourishing coat of creeper that almost hides its frontage. Inside, the bar and dining area combine traditional and contemporary features, creating a very pleasant, civilised ambience for enjoying a glass of ale and some good conversation. The food here is excellent, and the printed menu of classics like garlic mushrooms, burgers, battered haddock, home-made pies and sausage & mash is supplemented by a tempting list of blackboard specials; these might include calamari with a chilli dip, spicy Moroccan lamb and stuffed pork fillet with a mustard sauce. The Rising Sun is run by Oliver and Tristan Howard, sons of the owner of the inn since 1980.

---

116 Park Tavern

11 Priory Road, Chichester, Sussex PO19 1NS
Tel: 01243 785057

Real Ales, Bar Food, Restaurant Menu,
No Smoking Area

117 Prince Of Wales

The Gatehouse Lidsey Road, Chichester,
Sussex PO20 3ST
Tel: 01243 543247

Real Ales, Bar Food, Restaurant Menu,
No Smoking Area

118 Prince Of Wales Inn

Upper Bognor Road, Bognor Regis,
Sussex PO21 1JB
Tel: 01243 829633

Real Ales, No Smoking Area

119 The Queens Head

The Hollow, West Chiltington, Pulborough,
Sussex RH20 2JN
Tel: 01798 813143

Real Ales, Bar Food, Restaurant Menu,
No Smoking Area

120 The Railway

49-51 London Road, Bognor Regis,
Sussex PO21 1PR
Tel: 01243 828015

Real Ales, Bar Food, Accommodation,
Disabled Facilities

121 Rainbow Inn

56 St Pauls Road, Chichester, Sussex PO19 3BW
Tel: 01243 785867

Real Ales

122 The Red Lion

45 High Street, Arundel, Sussex BN18 9AG
Tel: 01903 882597

Real Ales, Bar Food, Restaurant Menu,
No Smoking Area, Disabled Facilities

123 Regis Brewers Fayre

The Esplanade, Bognor Regis, Sussex PO21 1PJ
Tel: 01243 841763

Restaurant Menu, No Smoking Area,
Disabled Facilities

124 Richmond Arms

Mill Road, West Ashling, Chichester, Sussex PO18 8EA
Tel: 01243 575730

Real Ales, Bar Food, Restaurant Menu,
Disabled Facilities

125 The Rising Sun

The Street, Nutbourne, Pulborough,
Sussex RH20 2HE
Tel: 01798 812191

Real Ales, Bar Food, Restaurant Menu,
No Smoking Area

See panel on page 107

126 The Robin Hood

Shripney Road, Shripney, Bognor Regis,
Sussex PO22 9PA
Tel: 01243 822323

Real Ales, Bar Food, Restaurant Menu,
Accommodation, No Smoking Area, Disabled Facilities

127 The Roundstone

Roundstone Lane, East Preston, Littlehampton,
Sussex BN16 1EB
Tel: 01903 785423

Bar Food, Restaurant Menu, No Smoking Area,
Disabled Facilities

128 Royal Hotel

The Esplanade, Bognor Regis, Sussex PO21 1SZ
Tel: 01243 864665

Bar Food, Restaurant Menu, Accommodation

129 Royal Norfolk Hotel

The Esplanade, Bognor Regis, Sussex PO21 2LH
Tel: 01243 826222

Real Ales, Bar Food, Restaurant Menu,
Accommodation, No Smoking Area, Disabled Facilities

130 Royal Oak

Pook Lane, East Lavant, Chichester, Sussex PO18 0AX
Tel: 01243 527434

Real Ales, Bar Food, Restaurant Menu,
Accommodation, No Smoking Area, Disabled Facilities

132 The Royal Oak

336 Chichester Road, North Bersted,
West Sussex PO21 5JF
☎ 01243 821002

Real Ales, Bar Food, Restaurant Menu,
No Smoking Area

- On the A259 Bognor Regis-Chichester road
- 2 cask ales
- 12-7
- Quiz 3 Thursdays a month, jam session the other Thursday
- Beer garden
- All day, every day
- Bognor Regis 1 mile, Chichester 3 miles

The Royal Oak is on a corner site on the A259 Chichester Road, a short drive out of Bognor Regis. In this most sociable Inn Janet and John Cattermole have created a warm and welcoming atmosphere. Open all day for two real ales and a full range of other drinks, the talented professional chef prepares excellent dishes served from noon to 7 o'clock every day.

131 Royal Oak
Hooksway, Chilgrove, West Sussex PO18 9JZ
Tel: 01243 535257
Real Ales, Bar Food, Restaurant Menu,
No Smoking Area, Disabled Facilities

132 **The Royal Oak**
336 Chichester Road, North Bersted,
Bognor Regis, Sussex PO21 5JF
Tel: 01243 821002
Real Ales, Bar Food, Restaurant Menu,
No Smoking Area

See panel opposite

133 The Royal Oak
Stocks Lane, Chichester, Sussex PO20 8BS
Tel: 01243 671010
Real Ales, Bar Food, Restaurant Menu,
No Smoking Area, Disabled Facilities

134 Rushmere Bar & Restaurant
Hillfield Road, Selsey, Chichester, Sussex PO20 9DB
Tel: 01243 605000
Real Ales, Bar Food, Restaurant Menu,
No Smoking Area, Disabled Facilities

135 The Seal
6 Seal Court Hillfield Road, Chichester,
Sussex PO20 0JX
Tel: 01243 602461
Real Ales, Bar Food, Restaurant Menu,
Disabled Facilities

136 Seaview Hotel
127 Sea Road, Littlehampton, Sussex BN16 1PD
Tel: 01903 773988
Real Ales, Bar Food, Restaurant Menu,
Accommodation, No Smoking Area, Disabled Facilities

137 The Selsey Arms
West Dean, Chichester, West Sussex PO18 0QX
Tel: 01243 811465
Real Ales, Bar Food, Restaurant Menu,
No Smoking Area

138 The Ship
Aldwick Street, Aldwick, Bognor Regis,
Sussex PO21 3AP
Tel: 01243 865334
Real Ales, Bar Food, Restaurant Menu,
No Smoking Area, Disabled Facilities

139 Ship & Anchor
Ford Marina, Ford, Arundel, Sussex BN18 0BJ
Tel: 01243 551747
Real Ales, Bar Food, No Smoking Area,
Disabled Facilities

140 Ship Hotel
North Street, Chichester, Sussex PO19 1NH
Tel: 01243 778000
Bar Food, Restaurant Menu, Accommodation,
No Smoking Area

141 Ship Inn
The Street, Itchenor, Chichester, Sussex PO20 7AH
Tel: 01243 512284
Real Ales, Bar Food, Restaurant Menu,
Accommodation, Disabled Facilities

142 Shoulder Of Mutton & Cucumbers
Main Road, Yapton, Arundel, Sussex BN18 0EU
Tel: 01243 551429
Real Ales, Bar Food, Restaurant Menu,
No Smoking Area, Disabled Facilities

143 **The Six Bells**
Lyminster Road, Lyminster, Littlehampton,
Sussex BN17 7PS
Tel: 01903 713639
Real Ales, Bar Food, Restaurant Menu,
No Smoking Area, Disabled Facilities

See panel on page 110

144 The Southdowns
133 Felpham Way, Felpham, Bognor Regis,
West Sussex PO22 8QJ
Tel: 01243 855834
Real Ales, Bar Food, Restaurant Menu,
No Smoking Area, Disabled Facilities

The Six Bells

168 Lyminster Road, Lyminster, Littlehampton,
West Sussex BN17 7PS

☎ 01903 713639 ⊕ www.sixbellslyminster.co.uk

**Real Ales, Bar Food, Restaurant Menu,
No Smoking Area, Disabled Facilities**

- By the A284 Lyminster and close to the A27
- Abbot Ale, London Pride
- 12-2.15 & 6.30-9.15
- Garden, patio, car park
- Major cards accepted
- No pets inside the inn (OK in the garden or patio)
- 11-3 & 6-11
- Arundel 3 miles, Littlehampton 1½ miles, Bognor 6 miles, Goodwood 5 miles, Fontwell 3 miles.

The Six Bells is a flint-faced old coaching inn with a history going back 300 years and a reputation under its current management for its food and its great atmosphere. Many original features have been retained in the public rooms, and the bar stocks a wide selection of ales, draught and bottled beers, lagers, wines, spirits and soft drinks.

Easily reached from the A27 road from Worthing to Arundel and Chichester, and a short drive from the coast at Littlehampton, the Six Bells has built up a loyal following for the quality of its cooking, and the interesting, wide-ranging menus cover everything from bar snacks to a full à la carte choice. Fresh ingredients, sourced locally as far as possible, are prepared with skill and care to produce excellent dishes such as three onion gorgonzola tart, maple roasted duck breast, sea bass, tuna niçoise, steak & ale pie, and chargrilled chicken caesar salad. A stylishly renovated flint barn provides the setting for a special occasion.

145 Sportsman

Rackham Road, Amberley, Arundel,
Sussex BN18 9NR
Tel: 01798 831787

Real Ales, Bar Food, Restaurant Menu,
Accommodation, No Smoking Area, Disabled Facilities

146 Spotted Cow

High Street, Littlehampton, Sussex BN16 4AW
Tel: 01903 783919

Real Ales, Bar Food, Restaurant Menu,
No Smoking Area

147 The Spotted Cow

Selsey Road, Hunston, Chichester,
Sussex PO20 2PD
Tel: 01243 786718

Real Ales, Bar Food, No Smoking Area,
Disabled Facilities

148 The Spur

London Road East, Slindon, Arundel,
Sussex BN18 0NE
Tel: 01243 814216

Real Ales, Bar Food, Restaurant Menu

149 St Marys Gate Inn

London Road, Arundel, Sussex BN18 9BA
Tel: 01903 883145

Real Ales, Bar Food, Restaurant Menu,
Accommodation, No Smoking Area

150 The Star And Garter

East Dean, Chichester, Sussex PO18 0JG
Tel: 01243 811318

Real Ales, Bar Food, Restaurant Menu,
Accommodation, No Smoking Area, Disabled Facilities

151 Suffolk House Hotel
3 East Row, Chichester, Sussex PO19 1PD
Tel: 01243 778899
Real Ales, Bar Food, Restaurant Menu,
Accommodation, No Smoking Area, Disabled Facilities

152 Sussex Brewery
36 Main Road, Hermitage, Emsworth,
Sussex PO18 8AU
Tel: 01243 371533
Real Ales, Bar Food, Restaurant Menu,
No Smoking Area, Disabled Facilities

153 The Swan
12-14 Westgate, Chichester, Sussex PO19 3EU
Tel: 01243 539336
Real Ales, Bar Food, No Smoking Area

154 The Swan
16 Chichester Road, Arundel, Sussex BN18 0AD
Tel: 01903 882677
Real Ales, Bar Food, Restaurant Menu,
Accommodation, No Smoking Area, Disabled Facilities

155 The Swan Bar & Restaurant
19 Swan Corner, Pulborough, West Sussex RH20 1RJ
Tel: 01798 873999
Real Ales, Bar Food, Restaurant Menu,
No Smoking Area, Disabled Facilities

156 Swan Hotel
27-29 High Street, Arundel, Sussex BN18 9AG
Tel: 01903 882314
Real Ales, Bar Food, Restaurant Menu,
Accommodation, No Smoking Area, Disabled Facilities

157 Swan Inn
Lower Street, Fittleworth, Pulborough,
Sussex RH20 1EN
Tel: 01798 865429
Real Ales, Bar Food, Restaurant Menu,
Accommodation, No Smoking Area

158 Thatched House Inn
8 Limmer Lane, Felpham, Bognor Regis,
West Sussex PO22 7EJ
Tel: 01243 865953
Real Ales

159 The Thatched Tavern
Church Road, East Wittering, Chichester,
Sussex PO20 8PU
Tel: 01243 673087
Real Ales, Bar Food
See panel on page 112

160 The Tudor Tavern
138-140 Sea Road, Littlehampton, Sussex BN16 1NN
Tel: 01903 773992
Real Ales

161 Unicorn Hotel
76 High Street, Bognor Regis, Sussex PO21 1RZ
Tel: 01243 865536
Real Ales

162 The Unicorn Inn
Heyshott, Midhurst, Sussex GU29 0DL
Tel: 01730 813486
Real Ales, Bar Food, Restaurant Menu,
No Smoking Area, Disabled Facilities

163 Victoria Inn
West Marden, Chichester, Sussex PO18 9EN
Tel: 02392 631330
Real Ales, Bar Food, Restaurant Menu,
Accommodation, No Smoking Area

164 Waverley Freehouse
6 Nyewood Lane, Bognor Regis, Sussex PO21 2QB
Tel: 01243 823137
Real Ales, Bar Food, Restaurant Menu,
No Smoking Area, Disabled Facilities

165 Wests
West Street, Chichester, Sussex PO19 1QU
Tel: 01243 539637
Bar Food, Restaurant Menu, No Smoking Area,
Disabled Facilities

159 The Thatched Tavern

Church Road, East Wittering, nr Chichester,
West Sussex PO20 8PU

☎ 01243 673087

Real Ales, Bar Food

🍺 7 miles SW of Chichester – A286 then B2198

🍺 Bombardier, Greene King IPA, Guest Ale

🍴 12-2.30 & 6-9.30 (Tues to 8, Sun 12-3 & 6-8.30)

🎵 Quiz Tues, live music weekly in summer, monthly in winter

🎪 Beer garden, car park

💳 Major cards accepted

🕐 11.30-3 & 6-9.30

🏛 Selsey Bill 5 miles (country roads), Chichester 7 miles

The Thatched Tavern is a Grade I listed 16th century building of stone and plaster, its immaculate whitewashed, black-shuttered frontage topped by a marvellous thatched roof. Picnic benches are set out at the front

among lovely flowers and shrubs, and there's a pleasant beer garden at the side. The bar and dining areas are every bit as delightful as the exterior would suggest. The bar counter features some beautiful carved panels, and beams and Tiffany-style wall lights add to the delightful scene. Hosts Mandie and Graham welcome everyone as a friend – singles, couples, families, children, dogs – and it's a real pleasure to chat with the other customers over a glass of well-kept cask ale – Greene King IPA and Bombardier are the regulars, with

a rotating guest adding to the selection. An elegant archway leads from the bar into the restaurant, where diners can choose between dishes on the main menu and the blackboard list of daily changing specials. On the main menu are classics such as prawn cocktail, scampi, lasagne, steaks and cod in beer batter, while among the specials might be spiced shrimps on a lemon grass stick, steak & kidney or chicken & ham pie, grilled rainbow trout, or a vegetarian combo of spicy potato wedges, onion rings, breaded mushrooms or jalapeno peppers.

With its picture-postcard looks and lovely setting, the Thatched Tavern is a popular venue for parties, wedding receptions and all sorts of other special occasions. Mandie, Graham and their staff are happy to make individual arrangements for these get-togethers, including the hiring of a marquee. The inn lies just north of the village of East Wittering on the road that leads to the B2179 then the A286 for the short run to Chichester. The sea at Bracklesham Bay is a short stroll away, and Selsey Bill is a healthy walk along the beach or a drive through country roads by way of Earnley and Highleigh.

166 The Wheatsheaf

85 Hawthorn Road, Bognor Regis, Sussex PO21 2BE
Tel: 01243 843055

Real Ales, Bar Food, No Smoking Area,
Disabled Facilities

167 The White Hart

12 Queen Street, Arundel, Sussex BN18 9JG
Tel: 01903 882374

Real Ales, Bar Food, Restaurant Menu,
Accommodation, No Smoking Area, Disabled Facilities

See panel below

168 White Hart

Stopham Road, Stopham Bridge, Pulborough,
Sussex RH20 1DS
Tel: 01798 873321

Real Ales, Bar Food, Restaurant Menu,
No Smoking Area, Disabled Facilities

169 The White Horse

39 Chichester Road, Bognor Regis,
Sussex PO21 2XH
Tel: 01243 864523

Real Ales, Accommodation, Disabled Facilities

170 The White Horse

Graffham, Petworth, Sussex GU28 0NT
Tel: 01798 867331

Real Ales, Bar Food, Restaurant Menu,
No Smoking Area, Disabled Facilities

171 The White Horse Inn

Bury Common, Pulborough, Sussex RH20 1NS
Tel: 01798 831343

Real Ales, Bar Food, Disabled Facilities

---

167 The White Hart

12 Queen Street, Arundel, West Sussex BN18 9JG
☎ 01903 882374

Real Ales, Bar Food, Restaurant Menu, Accommodation, No Smoking Area, Disabled Facilities

☛ In the heart of Arundel, 1 min from the Castle
🍺 Harveys Best Bitter
🍴 12-2 (Fri/Sat to 3) & 6-9 (Fri/Sat to 10.30), all day summer Sunday; no food Mon/Tues Oct-Apr)
🛏 4 rooms en suite
⚴ Patio
🕐 All day every day
🏛 Arundel Castle, River Arun and other sights of Arundel on the doorstep

The historic town of Arundel brings visitors from far and wide, but it's not only the vast hilltop Castle that attracts them. The town has many other places of interest, and for those with an interest in good hospitality and fine food and drink the **White Hart** comes at the top of the list. Founded in 1790, this handsome redbrick pub has been maintained in excellent decorative order, complementing the first-rate hospitality provided by George and Carol Foord and their son Ryan. George and Ryan are both talented and experienced chefs, and their printed menu and daily specials board provide diners with plenty of choice. The fresh fish dishes are a popular speciality at the weekend, when booking is strongly recommended. Children are welcome up to 9 o'clock in the evening, and they even have their own menu. Four quiet, comfortable bedrooms with en suite showers are available all year round for overnight guests.

176 The Wickham Arms

102 Bognor Road, Chichester,
West Sussex PO19 7TW
☎ 01243 784782

Real Ales, Bar Food, No Smoking Area

- ☛ On the outskirts of Chichester on the road to Bognor
- 🍺 Gales Bitter + 2 guests
- 🍴 12-3 & 6-8
- ♫ Karaoke Friday, live music Saturday, meat raffle Sunday
- 🚗 Car park, patio garden
- 💳 Cash only
- 🕐 All day, every day
- 🏛 Chichester Cathedral and other places of interest 1 mile

Situated on the Bognor Road on the outskirts of Chichester. The **Wickham Arms** is a handsome mid-Victorian building

that really takes the eye with its flint-faced frontage and white-painted door and window surrounds. Inside, visitors are presented with a merry jumble of bric-a-brac in the public rooms, including brasses and badges, mugs and jugs, prints and pictures, books and trophies. Outside is a beer garden with plenty of benches, tables and chairs set under parasols – a very popular spot for barbecues throughout the summer months.

The Wickham Arms is a great spot for a

drink, with Gales Bitter and two guests heading the list, but an even better plan is to take time to relax over a meal. There's always a good atmosphere here, generated by Ian Hurry and his son, Jack, their staff and the customers. Ian has been in the trade for more than 30 years; he is very talented chef, and he has certainly passed his skills on to Jack. They share the cooking here, and the menu and specials board offer a very good selection of classic pub dishes served every lunchtime and evening. Soup, paté and prawn cocktail are the permanent, popular starters, while main courses run from a big breakfast to cottage pie, cold meat salads, cod & chips, bangers & mash, chilli con carne, chicken curry and roast pork and beef. To finish, perhaps Madeira sponge or fruit crumble. This is a very popular eating place, so booking is recommended for all meals; food can also be pre-ordered – a very useful facility for taking a planned break while on business or sightseeing, or for an early supper before a visit to Chichester Theatre.

On the social side, the Wickham Arms holds karaoke nights on Friday and live music evenings on Saturday; on Sunday there's a meat raffle.

172 The White Horse Inn
Mare Hill Road, Pulborough, Sussex RH20 2DY
Tel: 01798 872189

Real Ales, Bar Food, Restaurant Menu,
No Smoking Area

173 White Horse Inn
The High Street, Chilgrove, Chichester,
Sussex PO18 9HX
Tel: 01243 535219

Real Ales, Bar Food, Restaurant Menu,
Accommodation, No Smoking Area, Disabled Facilities

174 White Horse Inn
The Street, Sutton, Pulborough, Sussex RH20 1PS
Tel: 01798 869221

Real Ales, Bar Food, Restaurant Menu,
Accommodation, No Smoking Area, Disabled Facilities

175 White Swan
Station Road, Bosham, Sussex PO18 8NG
Tel: 01243 576086

Real Ales, Bar Food, Restaurant Menu,
No Smoking Area

176 The Wickham Arms
102 Bognor Road, Chichester, Sussex PO19 7TW
Tel: 01243 784782

Real Ales, Bar Food, No Smoking Area

See panel opposite

177 The Wilkes Head
Church Lane, Eastergate, Chichester,
Sussex PO20 2UT
Tel: 01243 543380

Real Ales, Bar Food, Restaurant Menu,
No Smoking Area, Disabled Facilities

179 The Woodman Arms
Hammerpot, Angmering, West Sussex BN16 4EU
☎ 01903 871240

Real Ales, Bar Food, Restaurant Menu, No Smoking Area, Disabled Facilities

☛ Just off the A27. When travelling east towards Worthing look for sign to pub on the left before the A280 turn-off

🍺 HSB, Gales

🍴 12-2.30 (Sun to 4) & 7-9; no food Sun eve

🅿 Car park

💳 Major cards accepted

🚫 No children in bar area

🕐 Lunchtime and evening

🏛 Worthing 3 miles, Arundel 4 miles

Brian and Karen Liston have made many friends since taking over the **Woodman Arms** at the beginning of 2004. The social hub of a tiny community not far from the coast, this delightful thatched inn has parts dating back to the 16th century, and beyond the neat little front garden the bar and restaurant are particularly attractive and inviting, with a log-burning stove in the winter months. The inn has earned a well-deserved reputation for the quality of its cooking, and the regular menu, supplemented by daily specials, is served every session except Sunday evening. All the pub classics feature on the main menu – including a selection of light bites – while the daily specials might include Garlic Mushrooms, fresh haddock in their own beer batter, or calves' liver & bacon. Booking is recommended on Friday and Saturday evenings, but reservations are not taken for Sunday lunch, so arrive early.

178 The Winterton Arms

Crockerhill, Chichester, Sussex PO18 0LH
Tel: 01243 773202

Real Ales, Bar Food, Restaurant Menu,
No Smoking Area, Disabled Facilities

179 The Woodman Arms

Hammerpot, Angmering, Littlehampton,
Sussex BN16 4EU
Tel: 01903 871240

Real Ales, Bar Food, Restaurant Menu,
No Smoking Area, Disabled Facilities

See panel on page 115

180 The Woolpack Inn

71 Fishbourne Road West, Chichester,
Sussex PO19 3JJ
Tel: 01243 782792

Real Ales, Bar Food, Restaurant Menu,
No Smoking Area

TRAVEL PUBLISHING ORDER FORM

To order any of our publications just fill in the payment details below and complete the order form. For orders of less than 4 copies please add £1 per book for postage and packing. Orders over 4 copies are P & P free.

Please Complete Either:

I enclose a cheque for £ [＿＿＿＿＿＿] made payable to *Travel Publishing Ltd*

Or:

Card No: [＿＿＿＿＿＿＿＿＿＿] Expiry Date: [＿＿＿＿＿]

Signature: [＿＿＿＿＿＿＿＿＿＿＿]

Name: [＿＿＿＿＿＿＿＿＿＿＿]

Address: [＿＿＿＿＿＿＿＿＿＿＿]

Tel no: [＿＿＿＿＿＿＿＿＿＿＿]

Please either send, telephone, fax or e-mail your order to:
Travel Publishing Ltd, 7a Apollo House, Calleva Park, Aldermaston, Berkshire RG7 8TN
Tel: 0118 981 7777   Fax: 0118 982 0077   e-mail: info@travelpublishing.co.uk

	Price	Quantity			Price	Quantity
HIDDEN PLACES REGIONAL TITLES				**COUNTRY PUBS AND INNS**		
Cornwall	£8.99	....		Cornwall	£5.99	....
Devon	£8.99	....		Devon	£7.99	....
Dorset, Hants & Isle of Wight	£8.99	....		Sussex	£5.99	....
East Anglia	£8.99	....		Wales	£8.99	....
Lake District & Cumbria	£8.99	....		Yorkshire	£7.99	....
Northumberland & Durham	£8.99	....		**COUNTRY LIVING RURAL GUIDES**		
Peak District	£8.99	....		East Anglia	£10.99	....
Sussex	£8.99	....		Heart of England	£10.99	....
Yorkshire	£8.99	....		Ireland	£11.99	....
HIDDEN PLACES NATIONAL TITLES				North East	£10.99	....
England	£11.99	....		North West	£10.99	....
Ireland	£11.99	....		Scotland	£11.99	....
Scotland	£11.99	....		South of England	£10.99	....
Wales	£11.99	....		South East of England	£10.99	....
HIDDEN INNS TITLES				Wales	£11.99	....
East Anglia	£7.99	....		West Country	£10.99	....
Heart of England	£7.99	....		**OTHER TITLES**		
North of England	£7.99	....		Off the Motorway	£11.99	....
South	£7.99	....				
South East	£7.99	....				
Wales	£7.99	....				
West Country	£7.99	....				
Yorkshire	£7.99	....				

Total Quantity: [＿＿＿＿＿]

Post & Packing: [＿＿＿＿＿]

Total Value: [＿＿＿＿＿]

HIDDEN PLACES GUIDES

Explore Britain and Ireland with *Hidden Places* guides - a fascinating series of national and local travel guides.

Packed with easy to read information on hundreds of places of interest as well as places to stay, eat and drink.

Available from both high street and internet booksellers

For more information on the full range of *Hidden Places* guides and other titles published by Travel Publishing visit our website on

www.travelpublishing.co.uk
or ask for our leaflet by phoning **0118-981-7777** or
emailing **info@travelpublishing.co.uk**

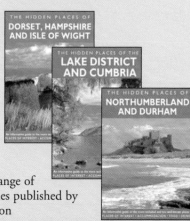

VISIT THE TRAVEL PUBLISHING WEBSITE

Looking for:
- *Places to Visit?*
- *Places to Stay?*
- *Places to Eat & Drink?*
- *Places to Shop?*

Then why not visit the Travel Publishing website...

- Informative pages on places to visit, stay, eat, drink and shop throughout the British Isles.

- Detailed information on Travel Publishing's wide range of national and regional travel guides.

www.travelpublishing.co.uk

Reader Reaction Form

The *Travel Publishing* research team would like to receive reader's comments on any pubs and inns covered (or not covered) in this guide so please do not hesitate to write to us using these reader reaction forms. We would also welcome recommendations for suitable entries to be included in the next edition. This will help ensure that the *Country Pubs and Inns series of Guides* continues to provide a comprehensive list of pubs and inns to our readers. To provide your comments or recommendations would you please complete the forms below and overleaf as indicated and send to:

**The Research Department, Travel Publishing Ltd,
7a Apollo House, Calleva Park, Aldermaston, Reading, RG7 8TN.**

Your Name:

Your Address:

Your Telephone Number:

Please tick as appropriate:

Comments ☐   Recommendation ☐

Name of Establishment:

Address:

Telephone Number:

Name of Contact:

Reader Reaction Form

Comment or Reason for Recommendation:

....

....

....

....

....

....

....

....

....

....

....

....

....

....

....

....

....

....